THE RA MATERIAL

The Law of One
BOOK III

The Law of One
Book III

DON ELKINS ↓ CARLA RUECKERT
JAMES ALLEN McCARTY

REDFeather™
MIND | BODY | SPIRIT

4880 Lower Valley Road, Atglen, PA 19310

Published by Red Feather Mind, Body, Spirit
An imprint of Schiffer Publishing, Ltd.
4880 Lower Valley Road
Atglen, PA 19310
Phone: (610) 593–1777; Fax: (610) 593–2002
E-mail: Info@schifferbooks.com
Web: www.redfeathermbs.com

For our complete selection of fine books on this and related subjects, please visit our
website at www.schifferbooks.com. You may also write for a free catalog.

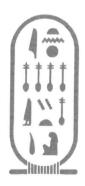

FOREWORD

On January 15, 1981, our research group started receiving a communication from the social memory complex Ra. From this communication precipitated the Law of One and some of the distortions of the Law of One.

The pages of this book contain an exact transcript, edited only to remove some personal material, of the communications received in Sessions 51 through 75 with Ra.

This material presupposes a point of view that we have developed in the course of many years' study of the UFO phenomenon. If you are not familiar with our previous work, a reading of our book *Secrets of the UFO* might prove helpful in understanding the present material. Also, as you can see from this book's title, there are 50 previous sessions with Ra that were collected in *The Law of One* and Book II of *The Law of One*. If at all possible, it is good to begin with the beginning with this material, since concepts build upon previous concepts. The Ra contact continued for 106 sessions, which were printed into four books in *The Law of One* series. They are available at your local bookstore, from Schiffer Publishing, or from us. If you wish to receive our quarterly newsletter, in which the best of our current channeling is published, please request that you be put on our mailing list.

Book III of *The Law of One* is an intensive study of the techniques of balancing of the energy centers and efficient polarization as our planet makes ready for harvest into fourth density. The nature of time/space and space/time is examined, and some of the ramifications of meditation and magic are discussed. A good deal of material about psychic attack and the Orion group is included, and the volume ends with a beginning glance into the archetypical mind.

L/L Research
Louisville, Kentucky
March 17, 1982

Session 51,
May 13, 1981

RA: I am Ra. I greet you in the love and in the light of the One Infinite Creator. We communicate now.

QUESTIONER: As we begin Book III of *The Law of One*, there are a couple of questions of fairly nontransient importance that I have, and one that I consider to be of a transient nature that I feel obligated to ask.

The first is clearing up the final point about harvest. I was wondering if there is a supervision over the harvest, and if so, why this supervision is necessary and how it works since an entity's harvestability is determined by the violet ray? Is it necessary for entities to supervise the harvest, or is it automatic?

RA: I am Ra. In time of harvest there are always harvesters. The fruit is formed as it will be, but there is some supervision necessary to ensure that this bounty is placed as it should be without the bruise or the blemish.

There are those of three levels watching over harvest.

The first level is planetary and that which may be called angelic. This type of guardian includes the mind/body/spirit complex totality or Higher Self of an entity and those inner plane entities which have been attracted to this entity through its inner seeking.

The second class of those who ward this process are those of the Confederation who have the honor/duty of standing in the small places at the edge of the steps of light/love so that those entities being harvested will not, no matter how confused or unable to make contact with their Higher Self, stumble and fall away for any reason other than the strength of the light. These Confederation entities catch those who stumble and set them aright so that they may continue into the light.

The third group watching over this process is that group you call the Guardians. This group is from the octave above our own and serves in this manner as light bringers. These Guardians provide the precise emissions of light/love in exquisitely fastidious disseminations of discrimination so that the precise light/love vibration of each entity may be ascertained.

Thus the harvest is automatic in that those harvested will respond according to that which is unchangeable during harvest. That is the violet-ray emanation. However, these helpers are around to ensure a proper harvesting so that each entity may have the fullest opportunity to express its violet-ray selfhood.

QUESTIONER: This next question I feel to be a transient type of question; however, it has been asked me by one whom I have communicated with who has been involved intensely in the UFO portion of the phenomenon. If you deem it too transient or unimportant, we'll skip it, but I have been asked how it is possible for the craft of the fourth density to get here since it seems that as you approach the velocity of light, the mass approaches infinity. My question would be why craft would be necessary at all?

RA: I am Ra. You have asked several questions. We shall respond in turn.

Firstly, we agree that this material is transient.

Secondly, those for the most part coming from distant points, as you term them, do not need craft as you know them. The query itself requires understanding which you do not possess. We shall attempt to state what may be stated.

Firstly, there are a few third-density entities who have learned how to use craft to travel between star systems while experiencing the limitations you now understand. However, such entities have learned to use hydrogen in a way different from your understanding now. These entities still take quite long durations of time, as you measure it, to move about. However, these entities are able to use hypothermia to slow the physical and mental complex processes in order to withstand the duration of flight. Those such as are from Sirius are of this type. There are two other types.

One is the type which, coming from fourth, fifth, or sixth density in your own galaxy, has access to a type of energy system which uses the speed of light as a slingshot and thus arrives where it wishes without any perceptible time elapsed in your view.

The other type of experience is that of fourth, fifth, and sixth densities of other galaxies and some within your own galaxy which have learned the necessary disciplines of personality to view the universe as one being and, therefore, are able to proceed from locus to locus by thought alone, materializing the necessary craft, if you will, to enclose the light body of the entity.

QUESTIONER: I assume that that latter type is the type we experience with the landings of the Orion group. Is this correct?

RA: I am Ra. The Orion group is mixed between the penultimate and the latter groups.

QUESTIONER: Why is a vehicle necessary for this transition? When you, as Ra, went to Egypt earlier you used bell-shaped craft, but you did this by thought. Can you tell me why you used a vehicle rather than just materializing the body?

RA: I am Ra. The vehicle or craft is that thought-form upon which our concentration may function as motivator. We would not choose to use our mind/body/spirit complexes as the focus for such a working.

QUESTIONER: Thank you. It seems to me, and you can tell me where I am going wrong with this statement, that we have seven bodies each corresponding to one of the seven colors of the spectrum and that energy that creates these seven bodies is a universal type of energy that streams into our planetary environment and comes in through the seven energy centers that we have called chakras to develop and perfect these bodies. Each of these bodies is somehow related to the mental configuration that we have, and the perfection of these bodies and the total instreaming of this energy is a function of this mental configuration, and through this mental configuration we may block, to some extent, the instreamings of energy that created these seven bodies. Could you comment on where I am wrong, and correct that which I have stated?

RA: I am Ra. Your statement is substantially correct. To use the term "mental configuration" is to oversimplify the manners of blockage of instreaming which occur in your density. The mind complex has a relationship to the spirit and body complexes which is not fixed. Thus blockages may occur betwixt spirit and mind, or body and mind, upon many different levels. We reiterate that each energy center has seven sub-colors, let us say, for convenience. Thus spiritual/mental blockages combined with mental/bodily blockages may affect each of the energy centers in several differing ways. Thus you may see the subtle nature of the balancing and evolutionary process.

QUESTIONER: I am unsure as to whether this will provide an avenue of questioning that will be fruitful, but I will ask this question since it seems to me that there is a connection here.

On the back of the book *Secrets of the Great Pyramid*, there are several reproductions of Egyptian drawings or works, some showing birds flying over horizontal entities. Could you tell me what this is and if it has any relationship to Ra?

RA: I am Ra. These drawings of which you speak are some of many which distort the teaching of our perception of death as the gateway to further experience. The distortions concern those considerations of specific nature as to processes of the so-called "dead" mind/body/ spirit complex. This may be termed, in your philosophy, the distortion of Gnosticism: that is, the belief that one may achieve knowledge and a proper position by means of carefully perceived and accentuated movements, concepts, and symbols. In fact, the process of the physical death is as we have described before: one in which there is aid available, and the only need at death is the releasing of that entity from its body by those around it and the praising of the process by those who grieve. By these means may the mind/body/spirit which has experienced physical death be aided, not by the various perceptions of careful and repeated rituals.

QUESTIONER: You spoke at an earlier time of rotational speeds of energy centers. Am I correct in assuming that this is a function of the blockage of the energy center, so that when it is less blocked, the speed of rotation is higher and the energy instreaming is greater?

RA: I am Ra. You are partially correct. In the first three energy centers a full unblocking of this energy will create speeds of rotation. As the entity develops the higher energy centers, however, these centers will then begin to express their nature by forming crystal structures. This is the higher or more balanced form of activation of energy centers as the space/time nature of this energy is transmuted to the time/ space nature of regularization and balance.

QUESTIONER: What do you mean by crystal structures?

RA: I am Ra. Each of the energy centers of the physical complex may be seen to have a distinctive crystalline structure in the more developed entity. Each will be somewhat different; just as in your world, no two snowflakes are alike. However, each is regular. The red energy center often is in the shape of the spoked wheel. The orange energy center in the flower shape containing three petals.

The yellow center again in a rounded shape, many faceted, as a star.

The green energy center sometimes called the lotus shape, the number of points of crystalline structure dependent upon the strength of this center.

The blue energy center capable of having perhaps one hundred facets and capable of great flashing brilliance.

The indigo center a more quiet center which has the basic

triangular or three-petalled shape in many, although some adepts who have balanced the lower energies may create more faceted forms.

The violet energy center is the least variable and is sometimes described in your philosophy as thousand petaled, as it is the sum of the mind/body/spirit complex distortion totality.

QUESTIONER: Right now I feel a feeling at the indigo center. If this center were totally activated and not blocked at all, would I then feel nothing there?

RA: I am Ra. This query, if answered, would infringe upon the Law of Confusion.

QUESTIONER: Immediately after the death of the physical body you have stated that the primary activated body is the indigo, and you stated that it is the form-maker. Why is this so?

RA: I am Ra. This will be the last full query of this session of working.

The indigo body may be seen to be an analog for intelligent energy. It is, in microcosm, the Logos. The intelligent energy of the mind/body/spirit complex totality draws its existence from intelligent infinity or the Creator. This Creator is to be understood, both in macrocosm and microcosm, to have, as we have said, two natures: the unpotentiated infinity which is intelligent; this is all that there is.

Free will has potentiated, both the Creator of us all and our selves, as co-Creators with intelligent infinity which has will. This will may be drawn upon by the indigo or form-making body, and its wisdom used to then choose the appropriate locus and type of experience which this co-Creator or sub-sub-Logos you call so carelessly a person will take.

I am Ra. This is the time for any brief queries.

QUESTIONER: Is there anything that we can do to make the instrument more comfortable or to improve the contact?

RA: I am Ra. All is well. You are conscientious. I leave you now, my brothers, in the love and in the light of the One Infinite Creator. Go forth, then, rejoicing in the power and the peace of the One Infinite Creator. Adonai.

Session 52,
May 19, 1981

RA: I am Ra. I greet you in the love and in the light of the One Infinite Creator. We communicate now.

QUESTIONER: In the previous session you stated: "The other type of experience is the fourth, fifth, and sixth densities of other galaxies, and some within your own galaxy which have learned necessary disciplines of personality to view the universe as one being are able to proceed from locus to locus by thought alone, materializing the necessary craft." I would like to ask you when you say fourth, fifth, and sixth densities of other galaxies, some within your own galaxy, are you stating here that more of the entities in other galaxies have developed the abilities of personality than have those in this galaxy for this type of travel? I am using the term "galaxy" with respect to the lenticular shape of billions of stars.

RA: I am Ra. We have once again used a meaning for this term, galaxy, that does not lie within your vocabulary at this time, if you will call it so. We referred to your star system.

It is incorrect to assume that other star systems are more able to manipulate the dimensions than your own. It is merely that there are many other systems besides your own.

QUESTIONER: Thank you. I think that possibly I am on an important point here because it seems to me that the great work in evolution is the discipline of personality, and it seems that we have two types of entities moving around the universe, one stemming from disciplines of personality, and the other stemming from what you call the slingshot effect. I won't even get into the sub-light speeds because I don't consider that too important. I only consider this material important because of the fact that we are considering disciplines of the personality.

Is the use of the slingshot effect for travel what you might call an intellectual or a left-brain type of involvement of understanding rather than a right brain type?

RA: I am Ra. Your perception on this point is extensive. You penetrate the outer teaching. We prefer not to utilize the terminology of right and left brain due to the inaccuracies of this terminology. Some functions are repetitive or redundant in both lobes, and further, to some entities the functions of the right and left are reversed. However, the heart of the query is worth some consideration.

The technology of which you, as a social complex, are so enamored at this time is but the birthing of the manipulation of the intelligent energy of the sub-Logos which, when carried much further, may evolve into technology capable of using the gravitic effects of which we spoke.

We note that this term is not accurate, but there is no closer term. Therefore, the use of technology to manipulate that outside the self is far, far less of an aid to personal evolution than the disciplines of the mind/body/spirit complex resulting in the whole knowledge of the self in the microcosm and macrocosm.

To the disciplined entity, all things are open and free. The discipline which opens the universes opens also the gateways to evolution. The difference is that of choosing either to hitchhike to a place where beauty may be seen, or to walk, step by step, independent and free in this independence to praise the strength to walk and the opportunity for the awareness of beauty.

The hitchhiker, instead, is distracted by conversation and the vagaries of the road and, dependent upon the whims of others, is concerned to make the appointment in time. The hitchhiker sees the same beauty but has not prepared itself for the establishment, in the roots of mind, of the experience.

QUESTIONER: I would ask this question in order to understand the mental disciplines and how they evolve. Does fourth-, fifth-, and sixth-density positive or service-to-others orientation of social memory complexes use both the slingshot and the personality disciplines type of effect for travel, or do they use only one?

RA: I am Ra. The positively oriented social memory complex will be attempting to learn the disciplines of mind, body, and spirit. However, there are some which, having the technology available to use intelligent energy forces to accomplish travel, do so while learning the more appropriate disciplines.

QUESTIONER: Then I am assuming that in the more positively oriented social memory complexes, a much higher percentage of them use the personality disciplines for this travel. Is this correct?

RA: I am Ra. This is correct. As positive fifth density moves into sixth there are virtually no entities which any longer use outer technology for travel or communication.

QUESTIONER: Could you give me the same information on the negatively oriented social memory complexes as to the ratios and as to how they use the slingshot effect or the disciplines of the personality for travel?

RA: I am Ra. The fourth-density negative uses the slingshot gravitic light effect, perhaps 80 percent of its membership being unable to master the disciplines necessary for alternate methods of travel. In fifth-density negative, approximately 50 percent at some point gain the necessary discipline to use thought to accomplish travel. As the sixth density approaches, the negative orientation is thrown into confusion and little travel is attempted. What travel is done is perhaps 73 percent of light/thought.

QUESTIONER: Is there any difference close to the end of fifth density in the disciplines of personality between positive and negative orientation?

RA: I am Ra. There are patent differences between the polarities but no difference whatsoever in the completion of the knowledge of the self necessary to accomplish this discipline.

QUESTIONER: Am I correct, then, in assuming that discipline of the personality, knowledge of self, and control in strengthening of the will would be what any fifth-density entity would see as those things of importance?

RA: I am Ra. In actuality these things are of importance in third through early seventh densities. The only correction in nuance that we would make is your use of the word "control." It is paramount that it be understood that it is not desirable or helpful to the growth of the understanding, may we say, of an entity by itself to control thought processes or impulses except where they may result in actions not consonant with the Law of One. Control may seem to be a shortcut to discipline, peace, and illumination. However, this very control potentiates and necessitates the further incarnative experience in order to balance this control or repression of that self which is perfect.

Instead, we appreciate and recommend the use of your second verb in regard to the use of the will. Acceptance of self, forgiveness of self, and the direction of the will; this is the path towards the disciplined personality. Your faculty of will is that which is powerful within you as co-Creator. You cannot ascribe to this faculty too much importance. Thus it must be carefully used and directed in service to others for those upon the positively oriented path.

There is great danger in the use of the will as the personality becomes stronger, for it may be used even subconsciously in ways reducing the polarity of the entity.

QUESTIONER: I sense, possibly, a connection between what you just said and why so many Wanderers have selected the harvest time on this planet to incarnate. Am I correct?

RA: I am Ra. It is correct that in the chance to remember that which has been lost in the forgetting, there is a nimiety of opportunity for positive polarization. We believe this is the specific thrust of your query. Please ask further if it is not.

QUESTIONER: I would just include the question as to why the time of harvest is selected by so many Wanderers as time for incarnation?

RA: I am Ra. There are several reasons for incarnation during harvest. They may be divided by the terms "self" and "other-self."

The overriding reason for the offering of these Brothers and Sisters of Sorrow in incarnative states is the possibility of aiding other-selves by the lightening of the planetary consciousness distortions and the probability of offering catalyst to other-selves which will increase the harvest.

There are two other reasons for choosing this service which have to do with the self.

The Wanderer, if it remembers and dedicates itself to service, will polarize much more rapidly than is possible in the far more etiolated realms of higher-density catalyst.

The final reason is within the mind/body/spirit totality or the social memory complex totality which may judge that an entity or members of a societal entity can make use of third-density catalyst to recapitulate a learning/teaching which is adjudged to be less than perfect. This especially applies to those entering into and proceeding through sixth density, wherein the balance between compassion and wisdom is perfected.

QUESTIONER: Thank you. Just as something that I am a little inquisitive about, but which is not of much importance, I would like to make a statement that I intuitively hunch. I may be wrong.

You were speaking of the slingshot effect, and that term has puzzled me.

The only thing that I can see is that you must put energy into a craft until it approaches the velocity of light, and this of course requires more and more energy. The time dilation occurs, and it seems to me that it would be possible to, by moving at 90° to the direction of travel, somehow change this stored energy in its application of direction or sense so that you move out of space/time into time/space with a 90° deflection. Then the energy would be taken out in time/space and you would reenter space/time at the end of this energy burst. Am I in any way correct on this?

RA: I am Ra. You are quite correct as far as your language may take you and, due to your training, more able than we to express the concept. Our only correction, if you will, would be to suggest that the 90° of which you speak are an angle which may best be understood as a portion of a tesseract.

QUESTIONER: Thank you. Just a little point that was bothering me, of no real importance.

Is there then, from the point of view of an individual who wishes to follow the service-to-others path, anything of importance other than disciplines of personality, knowledge of self, and strengthening of will?

RA: I am Ra. This is technique. This is not the heart. Let us examine the heart of evolution.

Let us remember that we are all one. This is the great learning/ teaching. In this unity lies love. This is a great learn/teaching. In this unity lies light. This is the fundamental teaching of all planes of existence in materialization. Unity, love, light, and joy; this is the heart of evolution of the spirit.

The second-ranking lessons are learn/taught in meditation and in service. At some point the mind/body/spirit complex is so smoothly activated and balanced by these central thoughts or distortions that the techniques you have mentioned become quite significant. However, the universe, its mystery unbroken, is one. Always begin and end in the Creator, not in technique.

QUESTIONER: In the previous session you mentioned the light bringers from the octave. Am I to understand that those who provide the light for the graduation are of an octave above the one we experience? Could you tell me more about these light bringers, who they are, etc.?

RA: I am Ra. This will be the last full query of this working.

This octave density of which we have spoken is both omega and alpha, the spiritual mass of the infinite universes becoming one central sun or Creator once again. Then is born a new universe, a new infinity, a new Logos which incorporates all that the Creator has experienced of Itself. In this new octave there are also those who wander. We know very little across the boundary of octave except that these beings come to aid our octave in its Logos completion. Is there any brief query which you have at this time?

QUESTIONER: Only is there anything that we can do to make the instrument more comfortable or to improve the contact?

RA: I am Ra. This instrument has some distortion in the area of the lungs which has been well compensated for by the position of the physical complex.

All is well.

We leave you, my friends, in the love and in the light of the One Infinite Creator. Go forth, therefore, rejoicing in the power and in the peace of the One Infinite Creator. Adonai.

Session 53,
May 25, 1981

RA: I am Ra. I greet you in the love and in the light of the One Infinite Creator. We communicate now.

QUESTIONER: I would first like to ask what is the instrument's condition, and then ask two questions for her. She would like to know if she can now do one exercise period per day, and also is the pain she feels prior to doing a session due to an Orion attack?

RA: I am Ra. The instrument's condition is as previously stated. In answer to the question of exercise, now that the intensive period is over, this instrument may, if it chooses, exercise one period rather than two. In scanning this instrument's physical complex distortions, we find the current period of exercise at the limit of this instrument's strength. This is well in the long run due to a cumulative building up of the vital energies. In the short run it is wearing to this entity. Thus we suggest the entity be aware of our previous admonitions regarding other aids to appropriate bodily distortions. In answer to the second query, we may say that the physical complex difficulties prior to contact with our social memory complex are due to the action of the subconscious will of the instrument. This will is extremely strong and requires the mind/body/spirit complex to reserve all available physical and vital energies for the contact. Thus the discomforts are experienced due to the dramatic distortion towards physical weakness while this energy is diverted. The entity is, it may be noted, also under psychic attack, and this intensifies preexisting conditions and is responsible for the cramping and the dizziness as well as mind complex distortions.

QUESTIONER: Thank you. I would like to know if [name] may attend one of these sessions in the very near future?

RA: I am Ra. The mind/body/spirit complex, [name], belongs with this group in the spirit and is welcome. You may request that special meditative periods be set aside until the entity sits with this working. We might suggest that a photograph of the one known as [name] be sent to this entity with his writing upon it indicating love and light. This held while meditating will bring the entity into peaceful harmony with each of you so that there be no extraneous waste of energy while greetings are exchanged between two entities, both of whom have a distortion towards solitude and shyness, as you would call it. The same might be done with a photograph of the entity, [name], for the one known as [name].

QUESTIONER: Thank you. During my trip to Laramie, certain things became apparent to me with respect to dissemination of the first book of the Law of One to those who have had experiences with UFOs and other Wanderers, and I will have to ask some questions now that I may have to include in Book I to eliminate a misunderstanding that I am perceiving as a possibility in Book I. Therefore, these questions, although for the most part transient, are aimed at eliminating certain distortions with respect to the understanding of the material in Book I. I hope that I am using the correct approach here. You may not be able to answer some of them, but that's all right. We'll just go on to others then if you can't answer the ones I ask.

Can you tell me of the various techniques used by the service-to-others positively oriented Confederation contacts with the people of this planet, the various forms and techniques of making contact?

RA: I am Ra. We could.

QUESTIONER: Would you do this please?

RA: I am Ra. The most efficient mode of contact is that which you experience at this space/time. The infringement upon free will is greatly undesired. Therefore, those entities which are Wanderers upon your plane of illusion will be the only subjects for the thought projections which make up the so-called Close Encounters and meetings between positively oriented social memory complexes and Wanderers.

QUESTIONER: Could you give me an example of one of these meetings between a social memory complex and a Wanderer as to what the Wanderer would experience?

RA: I am Ra. One such example of which you are familiar is that of the one known as Morris.*[1] In this case the previous contact which other entities in this entity's circle of friends experienced was negatively oriented. However, you will recall that the entity, Morris, was impervious to this contact and could not see, with the physical optical apparatus, this contact.

However, the inner voice alerted the one known as Morris to go by itself to another place, and there an entity with the thought-form shape and appearance of the other contact appeared and gazed at this entity, thus awakening in it the desire to seek the truth of this occurrence and of the experiences of its incarnation in general.

The feeling of being awakened or activated is the goal of this type of contact. The duration and imagery used varies depending upon the subconscious expectations of the Wanderer which is experiencing this opportunity for activation.

QUESTIONER: In a "Close Encounter" by a Confederation type of craft, I am assuming that this "Close Encounter" is with a thought-form type of craft. Have Wanderers within the past few years had "Close Encounters" with landed thought-form type of craft?

RA: I am Ra. This has occurred, although it is much less common than the Orion type of so-called Close Encounter. We may note that in a universe of unending unity, the concept of a "Close Encounter" is humorous, for are not all encounters of a nature of self with self? Therefore, how can any encounter be less than very, very close?

---

*1. This refers to Case #1 in *Secrets of the UFO* by D. T. Elkins with Carla L. Rueckert (Louisville, KY: L/L Research, 1976), pp. 10–11.

QUESTIONER: Well, talking about this type of encounter of self to self, have any Wanderers of a positive polarization ever had a so-called Close Encounter with the Orion or negatively oriented polarization?

RA: I am Ra. This is correct.

QUESTIONER: Why does this occur?

RA: I am Ra. When it occurs it is quite rare and occurs either due to the Orion entities' lack of perception of the depth of positivity to be encountered or due to the Orion entities' desire to, shall we say, attempt to remove this positivity from this plane of existence. Orion tactics normally are those which choose the simple distortions of mind which indicate less mental and spiritual complex activity.

QUESTIONER: I have become aware of a very large variation in the contact with individuals. Could you give me general examples of the methods used by the Confederation to awaken or partially awaken the Wanderers they contact?

RA: I am Ra. The methods used to awaken Wanderers are varied. The center of each approach is the entrance into the conscious and sub-conscious in such a way as to avoid causing fear and to maximize the potential for an understandable subjective experience which has meaning for the entity. Many such occur in sleep; others in the midst of many activities during the waking hours. The approach is flexible and does not necessarily include the "Close Encounter" syndrome as you are aware.

QUESTIONER: What about the physical examination syndrome. How does that relate to Wanderers and Confederation and Orion contacts?

RA: I am Ra. The subconscious expectations of entities cause the nature and detail of thought-form experience offered by Confederation thought-form entities. Thus if a Wanderer expects a physical examination, it will perforce be experienced with as little distortion towards alarm or discomfort as is allowable by the nature of the expectations of the subconscious distortions of the Wanderer.

QUESTIONER: Well, are those who are taken on both Confederation and Orion craft then experiencing a seeming physical examination?

RA: I am Ra. Your query indicates incorrect thinking. The Orion group uses the physical examination as a means of terrifying the individual and causing it to feel the feelings of an advanced second-density being such as a laboratory animal. The sexual experiences of some are a subtype of this experience. The intent is to demonstrate the control of the Orion entities over the Terran inhabitant.

The thought-form experiences are subjective and, for the most part, do not occur in this density.

QUESTIONER: Well, we have a large spectrum of entities on Earth with respect to harvestability, both positively oriented and negatively oriented. Would the Orion group target in on the ends of this spectrum, both positively and negatively oriented, for contact with Earth entities?

RA: I am Ra. This query is somewhat difficult to accurately answer. However, we shall attempt to do so.

The most typical approach of Orion entities is to choose what you might call the weaker-minded entity that it might suggest a greater amount of Orion philosophy to be disseminated.

Some few Orion entities are called by more highly polarized negative entities of your space/time nexus. In this case they share information just as we are now doing. However, this is a risk for the Orion entities due to the frequency with which the harvestable negative planetary entities then attempt to bid and order the Orion contact just as these entities bid planetary negative contacts. The resulting struggle for mastery, if lost, is damaging to the polarity of the Orion group.

Similarly, a mistaken Orion contact with highly polarized positive entities can wreak havoc with Orion troops unless these Crusaders are able to depolarize the entity mistakenly contacted. This occurrence is almost unheard of. Therefore, the Orion group prefers to make physical contact only with the weaker-minded entity.

QUESTIONER: Then in general we could say that if an individual has a "Close Encounter" with a UFO or any other type of experience that seems to be UFO related, he must look to the heart of the encounter and the effect upon him to determine whether it was Orion or Confederation contact. Is this correct?

RA: I am Ra. This is correct. If there is fear and doom, the contact was quite likely of a negative nature. If the result is hope, friendly feelings, and the awakening of a positive feeling of purposeful service to others, the marks of Confederation contact are evident.

QUESTIONER: Thank you. I did not wish to create the wrong impression with the material that we are including in Book I. I may find it necessary to add some of this material. As I say, I know that it is transient, but I believe it is necessary for a full understanding or, shall I say, a correct approach to the material.

I'll ask a few questions here, but if you do not care to answer them, we'll save them. I would like to ask, however, if you can tell me what, for the most part, the Confederation entities look like?

RA: I am Ra. The fourth-density Confederation entity looks variously depending upon the, shall we say, derivation of its physical vehicle.

QUESTIONER: Do some of them look just like us? Could they pass for Earth people?

RA: I am Ra. Those of this nature are most often fifth density.

QUESTIONER: I assume that the same answer would apply to the Orion group. Is this correct?

RA: I am Ra. This is correct.

Is there any other query of a brief nature we may answer?

QUESTIONER: I apologize for asking many transient questions during this session. I felt it necessary to include some of this material so that those Wanderers and others reading the first book of *The Law of One* would not get the wrong impression with respect to their experiences in contacts. I am sorry for any problems that I might have caused.

I will just ask if there is anything that we can do to aid the contact or to aid the instrument?

RA: I am Ra. The instrument is well. Please guard your alignments carefully. We leave you now, my friends, in the love and in the light of the One Infinite Creator. Go forth, therefore, rejoicing in the power and the peace of the Infinite Creator. Adonai.

Session 54,
May 29, 1981

RA: I am Ra. I greet you in the love and in the light of the One Infinite Creator. We communicate now.

QUESTIONER: I would like to trace the energy that I assume comes from the Logos. I will make a statement and let you correct me and expand on my concept.

From the Logos comes all frequencies of radiation of light. These frequencies of radiation make up all of the densities of experience that are created by that Logos. I am assuming that the planetary system of our sun, in all of its densities, is the total of the experience created by our sun as a Logos. Is this correct?

RA: I am Ra. This is correct.

QUESTIONER: I am assuming that the different frequencies are separated, as we have said, into the seven colors, and I am assuming that each of these colors may be the basic frequency for a sub-Logos of our sun Logos and that a sub-Logos or, shall we say, an individual may activate any one of these basic frequencies or colors and use the body that is generated from the activation of the frequency or color. Is this correct?

RA: I am Ra. If we grasp your query correctly, this is not correct in that the sub-sub-Logos resides not in dimensionalities, but only in co-Creators, or mind/body/spirit complexes.

QUESTIONER: What I meant was that a mind/body/spirit complex can then have any body activated that is one of the seven rays. Is this correct?

RA: I am Ra. This is correct in the same sense as it is correct to state that anyone may play a complex instrument which develops an euphonious harmonic vibration complex such as your piano and can play this so well that it might offer concerts to the public, as you would say. In other words, although it is true that each true color vehicle is available, potentially there is skill and discipline needed in order to avail the self of the more advanced or lighter vehicles.

QUESTIONER: I have made these statements to get to the basic question which I wish to ask. It is a difficult question to ask.

We have, coming from the sub-Logos we call our sun, intelligent energy. This intelligent energy is somehow modulated or distorted so that it ends up as a mind/body/spirit complex with certain distortions of personality which are necessary for the mind/body/spirit complex or mental portion of that complex to undistort in order to conform once more with the original intelligent energy.

First, I want to know if my statement on that is correct, and, secondly, I want to know why this is the way that it is and if there is any answer other than the first distortion of the Law of One for this?

RA: I am Ra. This statement is substantially correct. If you will penetrate the nature of the first distortion in its application of self knowing self, you may begin to distinguish the hallmark of an Infinite Creator, variety. Were there no potentials for misunderstanding and, therefore, understanding, there would be no experience.

QUESTIONER: OK. Once a mind/body/spirit complex becomes aware of this process, it then decides that in order to have the full abilities of the Creator it is necessary to reharmonize its thinking with the Original Creative Thought in precise vibration or frequency of vibration. In order to do this, it is necessary to discipline the personality so that it precisely conforms to the Original Thought, and this is broken into seven areas of discipline, each corresponding to one of the colors of the spectrum. Is this correct?

RA: I am Ra. This statement, though correct, bears great potential for being misunderstood. The precision with which each energy center matches the Original Thought lies not in the systematic placement of each energy nexus, but rather in the fluid and plastic placement of the balanced blending of these energy centers in such a way that intelligent energy is able to channel itself with minimal distortion.

The mind/body/spirit complex is not a machine. It is rather what you might call a tone poem.

QUESTIONER: Do all mind/body/spirit complexes in the entire creation have seven energy centers?

RA: I am Ra. These energy centers are in potential in macrocosm from the beginning of creation by the Logos. Coming out of timelessness, all is prepared. This is so of the infinite creation.

QUESTIONER: Then I will assume that the Creator in its intelligent appraisal of the ways of knowing Itself created the concept of the seven areas of knowing. Is this correct?

RA: I am Ra. This is partially incorrect. The Logos creates light. The nature of this light thus creates the nature of the catalytic and energetic levels of experience in the creation. Thus it is that the highest of all honor/duties, that given to those of the next octave, is the supervision of light in its manifestations during the experiential times, if you will, of your cycles.

QUESTIONER: I will make another statement. The mind/body/spirit complex may choose, because of the first distortion, the mental configuration that is sufficiently displaced from the configuration of the intelligent energy in a particular frequency or color of instreaming energy so as to block a portion of instreaming energy in that particular frequency or color. Is this correct?

RA: I am Ra. Yes.

QUESTIONER: Can you give me an idea of the maximum percentage of this energy it is possible to block in any one color?

RA: I am Ra. There may be, in an entity's pattern of instreaming energy, a complete blockage in any energy or color or combination of energies or colors.

QUESTIONER: OK. Then I assume that the first distortion is the motivator or what allows this blockage. Is this correct?

RA: I am Ra. We wish no quibbling but prefer to avoid the use of terms such as the verb "to allow." Free will does not allow, nor would predetermination disallow, experiential distortions. Rather the Law of Confusion offers a free reach for the energies of each mind/body/spirit complex. The verb "to allow" would be considered pejorative in that it suggests a polarity between right and wrong or allowed and not allowed. This may seem a minuscule point. However, to our best way of thinking it bears some weight.

QUESTIONER: Thank you. It bears weight to my own way of thinking also. I appreciate what you have told me.

Now, I would like to then consider the origin of catalyst. First we have the condition of mind/body/spirit complex, which, as a function of the first distortion, has reached a condition of blockage or partial blockage of one or more energy centers. I will assume that catalyst is necessary only if there is at least partial blockage of one energy center. Is this correct?

RA: I am Ra. No.

QUESTIONER: Could you tell me why?

RA: I am Ra. While it is a primary priority to activate or unblock each energy center, it is also a primary priority at that point to begin to refine the balances between the energies so that each tone of the chord of total vibratory beingness resonates in clarity, tune, and harmony with each other energy. This balancing, tuning, and harmonizing of the self is most central to the more advanced or adept mind/body/spirit complex. Each energy may be activated without the beauty that is possible through the disciplines and appreciations of personal energies or what you might call the deeper personality or soul identity.

QUESTIONER: Let me make an analogy that I have just thought of. A seven-stringed musical instrument may be played by deflecting each string a full deflection and releasing it, producing notes. Instead of producing the notes this way, the individual creative personality could deflect each string the proper amount in the proper sequence, producing music. Is this correct?

RA: I am Ra. This is correct. In the balanced individual the energies lie waiting for the hand of the Creator to pluck harmony.

QUESTIONER: I would like then to trace the evolution of catalyst upon the mind/body/spirit complexes and how it comes into use and is fully used to create this tuning. I assume that the sub-Logos that formed our tiny part of the creation, using the intelligence of the Logos of which it is a part, provides the base catalyst that will act upon mind/body complexes and mind/body/spirit complexes before they have reached a state of development where they can begin to program their own catalyst. Is this correct?

RA: I am Ra. This is partially correct. The sub-Logos offers the catalyst at the lower levels of energy, the first triad; these have to do with the survival of the physical complex. The higher centers gain catalyst from the biases of the mind/body/spirit complex itself in response to all random and directed experiences.

Thus the less developed entity will perceive the catalyst about it in terms of survival of the physical complex with the distortions which are preferred. The more conscious entity, being conscious of the catalytic process, will begin to transform the catalyst offered by the sub-Logos into catalyst which may act upon the higher-energy nexi. Thus the sub-Logos can offer only a basic skeleton, shall we say, of catalyst. The muscles and flesh having to do with the, shall we say, survival of wisdom, love, compassion, and service are brought about by the action of the mind/body/spirit complex on basic catalyst so as to create a more complex catalyst which may in turn be used to form distortions within these higher energy centers.

The more advanced the entity, the more tenuous the connection between the sub-Logos and the perceived catalyst, until, finally, all catalyst is chosen, generated, and manufactured by the self, for the self.

QUESTIONER: Which entities incarnate at this time on this planet would be in that category of manufacturing all of their catalyst?

RA: I am Ra. We find your query indeterminate but can respond that the number of those which have mastered outer catalyst completely is quite small.

Most of those harvestable at this space/time nexus have partial control over the outer illusion and are using the outer catalyst to work upon some bias which is not yet in balance.

QUESTIONER: In the case of service-to-self polarization, what type of catalyst would entities following this path program when they reach the level of programming their own catalyst?

RA: I am Ra. The negatively oriented entity will program for maximal separation from and control over all those things and conscious entities which it perceives as being other than the self.

QUESTIONER: A positively oriented entity may select a certain narrow path of thinking and activities during an incarnation and program conditions that would create physical pain if this were not followed. Is this correct?

RA: I am Ra. This is correct.

QUESTIONER: Would a negatively oriented entity do anything like this? Could you give me an example?

RA: I am Ra. A negatively oriented individual mind/body/spirit complex will ordinarily program for wealth, ease of existence, and the utmost opportunity for power. Thus many negative entities burst with the physical complex distortion you call health.

However, a negatively oriented entity may choose a painful condition in order to improve the distortion toward the so-called negative emotive mentations such as anger, hatred, and frustration. Such an entity may use an entire incarnative experience honing a blunt edge of hatred or anger so that it may polarize more towards the negative or separated pole.

QUESTIONER: Prior to incarnation, as an entity becomes more aware of the process of evolution and has selected a path whether it be positive or negative, at some point the entity becomes aware of what it wants to do with respect to unblocking and balancing its energy centers. At that point it is able to program for the life experience those catalytic experiences that will aid it in its process of unblocking and balancing. Is that correct?

RA: I am Ra. That is correct.

QUESTIONER: The purpose, then, of what we call the incarnate physical state seems to be wholly or almost wholly that of experiencing the programmed catalyst and then evolving as a function of that catalyst. Is that correct?

RA: I am Ra. We shall restate for clarity the purpose of incarnative existence is evolution of mind, body, and spirit. In order to do this, it is not strictly necessary to have catalyst. However, without catalyst the desire to evolve and the faith in the process do not normally manifest, and thus evolution occurs not. Therefore, catalyst is programmed and the program is designed for the mind/body/spirit complex for its unique requirements. Thus it is desirable that a mind/body/spirit complex be aware of and hearken to the voice of its experiential catalyst, gleaning from it that which it incarnated to glean.

QUESTIONER: Then it seems that those upon the positive path as opposed to those on the negative path would have precisely the reciprocal objective in the first three rays; red, orange, and yellow. Each path would be attempting to utilize the rays in precisely the opposite manners. Is this correct?

RA: I am Ra. It is partially and even substantially correct. There is an energy in each of the centers needed to keep the mind/body/spirit complex, which is the vehicle for experience, in correct conformation and composition. Both negative and positive entities do well to reserve this small portion of each center for the maintenance of the integrity of the mind/body/spirit complex. After this point, however, it is correct that the negative will use the three lower centers for separation from and control over others by sexual means, by personal assertion, and by action in your societies.

Contrary-wise, the positively oriented entity will be transmuting strong red-ray sexual energy into green-ray energy transfers and radiation in blue and indigo and will be similarly transmuting selfhood and place in society into energy transfer situations in which the entity may merge with and serve others and then, finally, radiate unto others without expecting any transfer in return.

QUESTIONER: Can you describe the energy that enters these energy centers? Can you describe its path from its origin, its form, and its effect? I don't know if this is possible.

RA: I am Ra. This is partially possible.

QUESTIONER: Would you please do that?

RA: The origin of all energy is the action of free will upon love. The nature of all energy is light. The means of its ingress into the mind/body/spirit complex is duple.

Firstly, there is the inner light which is Polaris of the self, the guiding star. This is the birthright and true nature of all entities. This energy dwells within.

The second point of ingress is the polar opposite of the North Star, shall we say, and may be seen, if you wish to use the physical body as an analog for the magnetic field, as coming through the feet from the earth and through the lower point of the spine. This point of ingress of the universal light energy is undifferentiated until it begins its filtering process through the energy centers. The requirements of each center and the efficiency with which the individual has learned to tap into the inner light determine the nature of the use made by the entity of these instreamings.

QUESTIONER: Does experiential catalyst follow the same path? This may be a dumb question.

RA: I am Ra. This is not a pointless question, for catalyst and the requirements or distortions of the energy centers are two concepts linked as tightly as two strands of rope.

QUESTIONER: You mentioned in an earlier session that the experiential catalyst was first experienced by the south pole and appraised with respect to its survival value. That's why I asked the question. Would you expand on this concept?

RA: I am Ra. We have addressed the filtering process by which incoming energies are pulled upwards according to the distortions of each energy center and the strength of will or desire emanating from the awareness of inner light. If we may be more specific, please query with specificity.

QUESTIONER: I'll make this statement, which may be somewhat distorted, and then let you correct it. We have, coming through the feet and base of the spine, the total energy that the mind/body/spirit complex will receive in the way of what we call light. Each energy center then filters out and uses a portion of this energy, red through violet. Is this correct?

RA: I am Ra. This is largely correct. The exceptions are as follows: The energy ingress ends with indigo. The violet ray is a thermometer or indicator of the whole.

QUESTIONER: As this energy is absorbed by the energy centers at some point, it is not only absorbed into the being but radiates through the energy center outwardly. I believe this begins at the blue center and also occurs in the indigo and violet? Is this correct?

RA: I am Ra. Firstly, we would state that we had not finished answering the previous query and may thus answer both in part by stating that in the fully activated entity, only that small portion of instreaming light needed to tune the energy center is used, the great remainder being free to be channeled and attracted upwards.

To answer your second question more fully, we may say that it is correct that radiation without the necessity of response begins with blue ray, although the green ray, being the great transitional ray, must be given all careful consideration, for until transfer of energy of all types has been experienced and mastered to a great extent, there will be blockages in the blue and indigo radiations.

Again, the violet emanation is, in this context, a resource from which, through indigo, intelligent infinity may be contacted. The radiation thereof will not be violet ray but rather green, blue, or indigo depending upon the nature of the type of intelligence which infinity has brought through into discernible energy.

The green-ray type of radiation in this case is the healing, the blue ray the communication and inspiration, the indigo that energy of the adept which has its place in faith.

QUESTIONER: What if a mind/body/spirit complex feels a feeling in meditation at the indigo center, what is he feeling?

RA: I am Ra. This will be the last full query of this working.

One who feels this activation is one experiencing instreamings at that energy center to be used either for the unblocking of this center, for its tuning to match the harmonics of its other energy centers, or to activate the gateway to intelligent infinity.

We cannot be specific, for each of these three workings is experienced by the entity which feels this physical complex distortion.

Is there a brief query before we leave this instrument?

QUESTIONER: I just would ask if there is anything that we can do to make the instrument more comfortable or to improve the contact?

RA: I am Ra. Please be aware of the need for the support of the instrument's neck. All is well. I leave you, my friends, in the love and in the light of the One Infinite Creator. Go forth, then, rejoicing in the power and the peace of the One Infinite Creator. Adonai.

Session 55,
June 5, 1981

RA: I am Ra. I greet you in the love and in the light of the One Infinite Creator. I communicate now.

QUESTIONER: I would first like to ask as to the condition of the instrument, please?

RA: I am Ra. This instrument is experiencing physical distortions toward weakness of the bodily complex occurring due to psychic attack. This instrument's vital energies have not been affected, however, due to the aid of those present in healing work. This instrument will apparently be subject to such weakness distortions due to incar-native processes which predispose the body complex towards weakness distortions.

QUESTIONER: Is there any specific thing that we can do that you have already told us or otherwise to alleviate this psychic attack or to help the instrument the most?

RA: I am Ra. We scan this instrument and find its distortion towards appreciation of each entity and each entity's caring, as you may call it. This atmosphere, shall we say, offers the greatest contrast to the discomfort of such psychic attacks, being the reciprocal, that is, the atmosphere of psychic support.

This each of you do as a subconscious function of true attitudinal, mental, emotional, and spiritual distortions towards this instrument. There is no magic greater than honest distortion toward love.

QUESTIONER: Thank you. I want to ask a couple questions about previous material that I didn't understand. I am hoping that this will clear up my understanding somewhat with respect to the mental con-figurations with which we have been dealing.

In the session before last, you stated, "However, this is a risk for the Orion entities due to the frequency with which the harvestable negative planetary entities attempt to bid and order the Orion contact just as these entities bid planetary negative contacts." Can you explain the mechanisms that affect polarization in consciousness with respect to this statement?

RA: I am Ra. The negative polarization is greatly aided by the subju-gation or enslavement of other-selves. The potential between two negatively polarized entities is such that the entity which enslaves the other or bids the other gains in negative polarity.

The entity so bidden or enslaved, in serving an other-self, will necessarily lose negative polarity although it will gain in desire for further negative polarization. This desire will then tend to create opportunities to regain negative polarity.

QUESTIONER: Am I to understand then that just the fact that the third-density entity calls or bids an Orion Crusader is a polarizing type of action that affects both entities?

RA: I am Ra. This is incorrect. The calling mechanism is not congruent in the slightest degree with the bidding mechanism. In the calling, the entity which calls is a suppliant neophyte asking for aid in negative understanding, if you may excuse this misnomer. The Orion response increases its negative polarity as it is disseminating the negative philosophy, thereby enslaving or bidding the entity calling.

There are instances, however, when the contact becomes contest, which is prototypical of negativity. In this contest, the caller will attempt not to ask for aid, but to demand results. Since the third-density negatively oriented harvestable entity has at its disposal an incarnative experiential nexus and since Orion Crusaders are, in a great extent, bound by the first distortion in order to progress, the Orion entity is vulnerable to such bidding if properly done. In this case, the third-density entity becomes master and the Orion Crusader becomes entrapped and can be bid. This is rare. However, when it has occurred, the Orion entity or social memory complex involved has experienced loss of negative polarity in proportion to the strength of the bidding third-density entity.

QUESTIONER: You mentioned that this will work when the bidding is properly done. What did you mean by "when the bidding is properly done"?

RA: I am Ra. To properly bid is to be properly negative. The percentage of thought and behavior involving service to self must approach 99 percent in order for a third-density negative entity to be properly configured for such a contest of bidding.

QUESTIONER: What method of communication with the Orion entity would a bidder of this type use?

RA: I am Ra. The two most usual types of bidding are, one, the use of perversions of sexual magic; two, the use of perversions of ritual magic. In each case the key to success is the purity of the will of the bidder. The concentration upon victory over the servant must be nearly perfect.

QUESTIONER: Can you tell me, in the polarizations in consciousness, if there is any analogy with respect to what you just said in this type of contact with respect to what we are doing right now in communicating with Ra?

RA: I am Ra. There is no relationship between this type of contact and the bidding process. This contact may be characterized as one typical of the Brothers and Sisters of Sorrow, wherein those receiving the contact have attempted to prepare for such contact by sacrificing extraneous, self-oriented distortions in order to be of service.

The Ra social memory complex offers itself also as a function of its desire to serve. Both the caller and the contact are filled with gratitude at the opportunity of serving others.

We may note that this in no way presupposes that either the callers or those of our group in any way approach a perfection or purity such as was described in the bidding process. The calling group may have many distortions and the working with much catalyst, as may those of Ra. The overriding desire to serve others, bonded with the unique harmonics of this group's vibratory complexes, gives us the opportunity to serve as one channel for the One Infinite Creator.

Things come not to those positively oriented but through such beings.

QUESTIONER: Thank you. You have stated in an earlier session that "until transfers of energy of all types have been experienced and mastered to a great extent, there will be blockages in the blue and in the indigo radiations." Could you explain that more fully?

RA: I am Ra. At this space/time we have not covered the appropriate intermediate material. Please requestion at a more appropriate space/time nexus.

QUESTIONER: I'm sort of hunting around here for an entry into some information. I may not be looking in a productive area.

You had stated that "as we (Ra) had been aided by shapes such as the pyramid, so we could aid your people." These shapes have been mentioned many, many times, and you have also stated that the shapes themselves aren't of too much consequence. I see a relation between these shapes and the energies that we have been studying with respect to the body, and I would like to ask a few questions on the pyramids to see if we might get an entry into some of this understanding.

You stated, "You will find the intersection of the triangle which is at the first level on each of the four sides forms a diamond in a plane which is horizontal." Can you tell me what you meant by the word "intersection"?

RA: I am Ra. Your mathematics and arithmetic have a paucity of configurative descriptions which we might use. Without intending to be obscure, we may note that the purpose of the shapes is to work with time/space portions of the mind/body/spirit complex. Therefore, the intersection is both space/time and time/space oriented and thus is expressed in three-dimensional geometry by two intersections which, when projected in both time/space and space/time, form one point.

QUESTIONER: I have calculated this point to be one-sixth of the height of the triangle that forms the side of the pyramid. Is this correct?

RA: I am Ra. Your calculations are substantially correct, and we are pleased at your perspicacity.

QUESTIONER: This would indicate to me that in the Great Pyramid at Giza, the Queen's Chamber, as it is called, would be the chamber used for initiation. Is this correct?

RA: I am Ra. Again, you penetrate the outer teaching.
The Queen's Chamber would not be appropriate or useful for healing work, as that work involves the use of energy in a more synergic configuration rather than the configuration of the centered being.

QUESTIONER: Then would the healing work be done in the King's Chamber?

RA: I am Ra. This is correct. We may note that such terminology is not our own.

QUESTIONER: Yes, I understand that. It is just that it is the common naming of the two chambers of the Great Pyramid. I don't know whether this line of questioning is going to take me to a better understanding of the energies, but until I have explored the concepts, there is nothing much that I can do but to ask a few questions.
There is a chamber below the bottom level of the pyramid, down below ground, that appears to be roughly in line with the King's Chamber. What is that chamber?

RA: I am Ra. We may say that there is information to be gained from this line of querying. The chamber you request to be informed about is a resonating chamber. The bottom of such a structure, in order to cause the appropriate distortions for healing catalyst, shall be open.

QUESTIONER: The book *The Life Force of the Great Pyramid* has related the ankh shape with a resonance in the pyramid. Is this a correct analysis?

RA: I am Ra. We have scanned your mind and find the phrase "working with crayons." This would be applicable. There is only one significance to these shapes such as the crux ansata; that is, the placing in coded form of mathematical relationships.

QUESTIONER: Is the 76° and 18' angle at the apex of the pyramid a critical angle?

RA: I am Ra. For the healing work intended, this angle is appropriate.

QUESTIONER: Why does the King's Chamber have the various small chambers above it?

RA: I am Ra. This will be the last full query of this working.

We must address this query more generally in order to explicate your specific question. The positioning of the entity to be healed is such that the life energies, if you will, are in a position to be briefly interrupted or intersected by light. This light then may, by the catalyst of the healer with the crystal, manipulate the aural forces, as you may call the various energy centers, in such a way that if the entity to be healed wills it so, corrections may take place. Then the entity is repro- tected by its own, now less distorted, energy field and is able to go its way.

The process by which this is done involves bringing the entity to be healed to an equilibrium. This involves temperature, barometric pressure, and the electrical-charged atmosphere. The first two require- ments are controlled by the system of chimneys.

QUESTIONER: Does this healing work by affecting the energy centers in such a way that they are unblocked so as to perfect the seven bodies that they generate and, therefore, bring the entity to be healed into proper balance?

RA: I am Ra. This entity tires. We must answer in brief and state simply that the distorted configuration of the energy centers is intended to be temporarily interrupted, and the opportunity is then presented to the one to be healed to grasp the baton, to take the balanced route and to walk thence with the distortions towards disease of mind, body, and spirit greatly lessened.

The catalytic effect of the charged atmosphere and the crystal directed by the healer must be taken into consideration as integral portions of this process, for the bringing back of the entity to a configuration of conscious awareness would not be accomplished after the reorganization possibilities are offered without the healer's presence and directed will. Are there any brief queries before we leave this instrument?

QUESTIONER: Only is there anything that we can do to make the instrument more comfortable or to improve this contact?

RA: I am Ra. All is well. You are conscientious. I now leave this working. I am Ra. I leave you, my friends, in the love and in the light of the One Infinite Creator. Go forth, then, rejoicing in the power and in the peace of the One Infinite Creator. Adonai.

Session 56,
June 8, 1981

RA: I am Ra. I greet you in the love and in the light of the One Infinite Creator. We communicate now.

QUESTIONER: Would you first please give me an indication of the instrument's condition?

RA: I am Ra. This instrument is severely distorted towards weakness of the mental and physical complexes at this time and is under psychic attack due to this opportunity.

QUESTIONER: Would it be better to discontinue the contact at this time?

RA: I am Ra. This is entirely at your discretion. This instrument has some energy transferred which is available. However, it is not great due to the effects as previously stated.

We, if you desire to question us further at this working, will as always attempt to safeguard this instrument. We feel that you are aware of the parameters without further elaboration.

QUESTIONER: In that case, I will ask how does the pyramid shape work?

RA: I am Ra. We are assuming that you wish to know the principle of the shapes, angles, and intersections of the pyramid at what you call Giza.

In reality, the pyramid shape does no work. It does not work. It is an arrangement for the centralization as well as the diffraction of the spiraling upward light energy as it is being used by the mind/body/ spirit complex.

The spiraling nature of light is such that the magnetic fields of an individual are affected by spiraling energy. Certain shapes offer an echo chamber, shall we say, or an intensifier for spiraling prana, as some have called this all-present, primal distortion of the One Infinite Creator.

If the intent is to intensify the necessity for the entity's own will to call forth the inner light in order to match the intensification of the spiraling light energy, the entity will be placed in what you have called the Queen's Chamber position in this particular shaped object. This is the initiatory place and is the place of resurrection.

The offset place, representing the spiral as it is in motion, is the appropriate position for one to be healed, as in this position an entity's vibratory magnetic nexi are interrupted in their normal flux. Thus a possibility/probability vortex ensues; a new beginning, shall we say, is offered for the entity in which the entity may choose a less distorted, weak, or blocked configuration of energy center magnetic distortions.

The function of the healer and crystal may not be overemphasized, for this power of interruption must needs be controlled, shall we say, with incarnate intelligence; the intelligence being that of one which recognizes energy patterns which, without judging, recognizes blockage, weakness, and other distortion and which is capable of visualizing, through the regularity of self and of crystal, the less distorted other-self to be healed.

Other shapes which are arched, groined, vaulted, conical, or, as your tipis, are also shapes with this type of intensification of spiraling light. Your caves, being rounded, are places of power due to this shaping.

It is to be noted that these shapes are dangerous. We are quite pleased to have the opportunity to enlarge upon the subject of shapes such as the pyramid, for we wish, as part of our honor/duty, to state that there are many wrong uses for these curved shapes; for with improper placement, improper intentions, or lack of the crystallized being functioning as channel for healing, the sensitive entity will be distorted more rather than less in some cases.

It is to be noted that your peoples build, for the most part, the cornered or square habitations, for they do not concentrate power. It is further to be noted that the spiritual seeker has, for many of your time periods of years, sought the rounded, arched, and peaked forms as an expression of the power of the Creator.

QUESTIONER: Is there an apex angle that is the angle for maximum efficiency in the pyramid?

RA: I am Ra. Again, to conserve this instrument's energy, I am assuming that you intend to indicate the most appropriate angle of apex for healing work. If the shape is such that it is large enough to contain an individual mind/body/spirit complex at the appropriate offset position within it, the 76° 18', approximate, angle is useful and appropriate. If the position varies, the angle may vary. Further, if the healer has the ability to perceive distortions with enough discrimination, the position within any pyramid shape may be moved about until results are effected. However, we found this particular angle to be useful. Other social memory complexes, or portions thereof, have determined different apex angles for different uses, not having to do with healing but with learning. When one works with the cone, or shall we say, the silo type of shape, the energy for healing may be found to be in a general circular pattern unique to each shape as a function of its particular height and width and in the cone shape, the angle of apex. In these cases, there are no corner angles. Thus the spiraling energy works in circular motion.

QUESTIONER: I will make a statement which you can correct. I intuitively see the spiraling energy of the Giza pyramid being spread out as it moves through the so-called King's Chamber and refocusing in the so-called Queen's Chamber. I am guessing that the spread of energy in the so-called King's Chamber is seen in the spectrum of colors, red through violet, and that the energy centers of the entity to be healed should be aligned with this spread of the spectrum so that the spectrum matches his various energy centers. Will you correct this statement?

RA: I am Ra. We can correct this statement.

QUESTIONER: Will you please do that?

RA: The spiraling energy is beginning to be diffused at the point where it goes through the King's Chamber position. However, although the spirals continue to intersect, closing and opening in double-spiral fashion through the apex angle, the diffusion or strength of the spiraling energies, red through violet color values, lessens, if we speak of strength, and gains, if we speak of diffusion, until at the peak of the pyramid you have a very weak color resolution useful for healing purposes. Thus the King's Chamber position is chosen as the first spiral after the centered beginning through the Queen's Chamber position. You may visualize the diffusion angle as the opposite of the pyramid angle, but the angle being less wide than the apex angle of the pyramid, being somewhere between 33° and 54°, depending upon the various rhythms of the planet itself.

QUESTIONER: Then I assume that if I start my angle at the bottom of the Queen's Chamber and make a 33° to 54° angle from that point, so that half of that angle falls on the side of the centerline that the King's Chamber is on, that will indicate the diffusion of the spectrum, starting from the point at the bottom of the Queen's Chamber; let's say, if we were using a 40° angle, we would have a 20° diffusion to the left of the centerline, passing through the King's Chamber. Is that correct?

RA: I am Ra. This will be the last full question of this session. It is correct that half of the aforementioned angle passes through the King's Chamber position. It is incorrect to assume that the Queen's Chamber is the foundation of the angle. The angle will begin somewhere between the Queen's Chamber position and thence downward towards the level of the resonating chamber, offset for the healing work.

This variation is dependent upon various magnetic fluxes of the planet. The King's Chamber position is designed to intersect the strongest spiral of the energy flow regardless of where the angle begins. However, as it passes through the Queen's Chamber position, this spiraling energy is always centered and at its strongest point.

May we answer any brief queries at this time?

QUESTIONER: I will just ask if there is anything that we can do to make the instrument more comfortable or to improve the contact?

RA: I am Ra. All is well, my friends. It is well, however, to be conscious of the limitations of this instrument. We feel the alignments are excellent at this time. I am Ra. I leave you in the love and in the light of the One Infinite Creator. Go forth, therefore, rejoicing in the power and in the peace of the One Infinite Creator. Adonai.

Session 57,
June 12, 1981

RA: I am Ra. I greet you in the love and in the light of the One Infinite Creator. We communicate now.

QUESTIONER: First, could you give me an indication of the instrument's condition, please?

RA: I am Ra. This instrument is under a most severe psychic attack. This instrument is bearing up well due to replenished vital energies and a distortion towards a sense of proportion which your peoples call a sense of humor.

This attack is potentially disruptive to this contact for a brief period of your space/time.

QUESTIONER: Is there anything in particular that we can do in addition to what we are doing to alleviate this attack? ·

RA: I am Ra. There is nothing you can do to alleviate the attack. The understanding of its mechanism might be of aid.

QUESTIONER: Could you tell us its mechanism?

RA: I am Ra. The Orion group cannot interfere directly but only through preexisting distortions of mind/body/spirit complexes.

Thus in this case, this entity reached for an heavy object with one hand, and this miscalculated action caused a deformation or distortion of the skeletal/muscular structure of one of this instrument's appendages.

Your aid may be helpful in supporting this instrument in the proper care of this distortion, which is equivalent to what you call your postoperative state when bones are not firmly knit. This instrument needs to be aware of care necessary to avoid such miscalculated actions, and your support in this state of awareness is noted and encouraged.

QUESTIONER: Is there anything that we can specifically do to alleviate this problem that is already existing?

RA: I am Ra. This information is harmless; thus we share it though it is transient, lacking the principle but only offering a specific transient effect.

The wrist area should be wrapped as in the sprained configuration, as you call this distortion, and what you call a sling may be used on this distorted right side of the body complex for one diurnal period. At that time, symptoms, as you call these distortions, shall be reviewed and such repeated until the distortion is alleviated.

The healing work to which each is apprentice may be used as desired.

It is to be noted that a crystal is available.

QUESTIONER: Which crystal is that?

RA: I am Ra. The flawed but sufficient crystal which rests upon the digit of this instrument's right hand.

QUESTIONER: Would you tell me how to use that crystal for this purpose?

RA: I am Ra. This is a large question.

You first, as a mind/body/spirit complex, balance and polarize the self, connecting the inner light with the upward spiraling inpourings of the universal light. You have done exercises to regularize the processes involved. Look to them for the preparation of the crystallized being.

Take then the crystal and feel your polarized and potentiated balanced energy channeled in green-ray healing through your being, going into and activating the crystalline regularity of frozen light which is the crystal. The crystal will resound with the charged light of incarnative love, and light energy will begin to radiate in specified fashion, beaming, in required light vibrations, healing energy, focused and intensified towards the magnetic field of the mind/body/spirit complex which is to be healed. This entity requesting such healing will then open the armor of the overall violet/red-ray protective vibratory shield. Thus the inner vibratory fields, from center to center in mind, body, and spirit, may be interrupted and adjusted momentarily, thus offering the one to be healed the opportunity to choose a less distorted inner complex of energy fields and vibratory relationships.

QUESTIONER: Should the crystal be held in the right hand of the healer?

RA: I am Ra. This is incorrect. There are two recommended configurations.

The first, the chain about the neck to place the crystal in the physical position of the green-ray energy center. Second, the chain hung from the right hand, outstretched, wound about the hand in such a way that the crystal may be swung so as to affect sensitive adjustments.

We offer this information realizing that much practice is needed to efficiently use these energies of self. However, each has the capability of doing so, and this information is not information which, if followed accurately, can be deleterious.

QUESTIONER: Would an unflawed crystal be considerably more effective than the flawed one that we have now?

RA: I am Ra. Without attempting to deem the priorities you may choose, we may note that the regularized or crystallized entity, in its configuration, is as critical as the perfection of the crystal used.

QUESTIONER: Does the physical size of the crystal have any relationship to the effectiveness in the healing?

RA: I am Ra. In some applications concerning planetary healing, this is a consideration. In working with an individual mind/body/spirit complex, the only requirement is that the crystal be in harmony with the crystallized being. There is perhaps a lower limit to the size of what you may call a faceted crystal, for light coming through this crystal needs to be spread the complete width of the spectrum of the one to be healed.

It may further be noted that water is a type of crystal which is efficacious also, although not as easy to hang from a chain in your density.

QUESTIONER: Placing the end of this pencil on my navel, would the point of it then represent the place where the crystal should hang for proper green ray? Is this position correct?

RA: I am Ra. We attempt your measurements. From 2 to 5.4 centimeters towards your heart is optimal.

QUESTIONER: Using this piece of wood, then, I would determine, from my navel, the position to be at the top of the piece of wood. Is this correct?

RA: I am Ra. This is correct.

QUESTIONER: How does the healing that you just told us about relate to the healing done in the King's Chamber in the Giza pyramid?

RA: I am Ra. There are two advantages to doing this working in such a configuration of shapes and dimensions.

Firstly, the disruption or interruption of the violet/red armoring or protective shell is automatic.

In the second place, the light is configured by the very placement of this position in the seven distinctive color or energy vibratory rates, thus allowing the energy through the crystallized being, focused with the crystal, to manipulate with great ease the undisturbed and, shall we say, carefully delineated palate of energies or colors, both in space/time and in time/space. Thus the unarmored being may be adjusted rapidly. This is desirable in some cases, especially when the armoring is the largest moiety of the possibility of continued function of body complex activity in this density. The trauma of the interruption of this armoring vibration is then seen to be lessened.

We take this opportunity to pursue our honor/duty, as some of those creating the pyramid shape, to note that it is in no way necessary to use this shape in order to achieve healings, for seniority of vibration has caused the vibratory complexes of mind/body/spirit complexes to be healed to be less vulnerable to the trauma of the interrupted armoring.

Furthermore, as we have said, the powerful effect of the pyramid, with its mandatory disruption of the armoring, if used without the crystallized being, used with the wrong intention, or in the wrong configuration, can result in further distortions of entities which are perhaps the equal of some of your chemicals which cause disruptions in the energy fields in like manner.

QUESTIONER: Is there currently any use for the pyramid shape at all that is beneficial?

RA: I am Ra. This is in the affirmative if carefully used.

The pyramid may be used for the improvement of the meditative state as long as the shape is such that the entity is in Queen's Chamber position or entities are in balanced configuration about this central point.

The small pyramid shape, placed beneath a portion of the body complex, may energize this body complex. This should be done for brief periods only, not to exceed thirty of your minutes.

The use of the pyramid to balance planetary energies still functions to a slight extent, but due to earth changes, the pyramids are no longer aligned properly for this work.

QUESTIONER: What is the aid or the mechanism of the aid received for meditation by an entity who would be positioned in the so-called Queen's Chamber position?

RA: I am Ra. Consider the polarity of mind/body/spirit complexes. The inner light is that which is your heart of being. Its strength equals your strength of will to seek the light. The position or balanced position of a group intensifies the amount of this will, the amount of awareness of the inner light necessary to attract the instreaming light upward spiraling from the south magnetic pole of being.

Thus this is the place of the initiate, for many extraneous items or distortions will leave the entity as it intensifies its seeking, so that it may become one with this centralized and purified incoming light.

QUESTIONER: Then if a pyramid shape is used, it would seem to me that it would be necessary to make it large enough so that the Queen's Chamber position would be far enough from the King's Chamber position so that you could use that energy position and not be harmed by the energy position of the King's Chamber position. Is this correct?

RA: I am Ra. In this application a pyramid shape may be smaller if the apex angle is less, thus not allowing the formation of the King's Chamber position. Also efficacious for this application are the following shapes: the silo, the cone, the dome, and the tipi.

QUESTIONER: Do these shapes that you just mentioned have any of the effect of the King's Chamber at all, or do they have only the Queen's Chamber effect?

RA: I am Ra. These shapes have the Queen's Chamber effect. It is to be noted that a strongly crystallized entity is, in effect, a portable King's Chamber position.

QUESTIONER: Then are you saying that there is absolutely no need, use, or good in having the King's Chamber effect at this time in our planetary evolution?

RA: I am Ra. If those who desired to be healers were of a crystallized nature and were all supplicants, those wishing less distortion, the pyramid would be, as always, a carefully designed set of parameters to distribute light and its energy so as to aid in healing catalyst.

However, we found that your peoples are not distorted towards the desire for purity to a great enough extent to be given this powerful and potentially dangerous gift. We, therefore, would suggest it not be used for healing in the traditional, shall we say, King's Chamber configuration which we naively gave to your peoples only to see its use grossly distorted and our teachings lost.

QUESTIONER: What would be an appropriate apex angle for a tipi shape for our uses?

RA: I am Ra. This is at your discretion. The principle of circular, rounded, or peaked shapes is that the center acts as an invisible inductive coil. Thus the energy patterns are spiraling and circular. Thus the choice of the most pleasant configuration is yours. The effect is relatively fixed.

QUESTIONER: Is there any variation in the effect with respect to the material of construction, the thickness of the material? Is it simply the geometry of the shape, or is it related to some other factors?

RA: I am Ra. The geometry, as you call it, or relationships of these shapes in their configuration is the great consideration. It is well to avoid stannous material or that of lead or other baser metals. Wood, plastic, glass, and other materials may all be considered to be appropriate.

QUESTIONER: If a pyramid shape were placed below an entity, how would this be done? Would it be placed beneath the bed? I'm not quite sure about how to energize the entity by "placing it below." Could you tell me how to do that?

RA: I am Ra. Your assumption is correct. If the shape is of appropriate size, it may be placed directly beneath the cushion of the head or the pallet upon which the body complex rests.

We again caution that the third spiral of upward-lining light, that which is emitted from the apex of this shape, is most deleterious to an entity in overdose and should not be used overlong.

QUESTIONER: What would the height be, in centimeters, of one of these pyramids for best functioning?

RA: I am Ra. It matters not. Only the proportion of the height of the pyramid from base to apex to the perimeter of the base is at all important.

QUESTIONER: What should that proportion be?

RA: I am Ra. This proportion should be the 1.16 which you may observe.

QUESTIONER: Do you mean that the sum of the four base sides should be 1.16 of the height of the pyramid?

RA: I am Ra. This is correct.

QUESTIONER: By saying that the Queen's Chamber was the initiatory place, could you tell me what you mean by that?

RA: I am Ra. This question is a large one. We cannot describe initiation in its specific sense due to our distortion towards the belief/understanding that the process which we offered so many of your years ago was not a balanced one.

However, you are aware of the concept of initiation and realize that it demands the centering of the being upon the seeking of the Creator. We have hoped to balance this understanding by enunciating the Law of One; that is, that all things are One Creator. Thus seeking the Creator is done not just in meditation and in the work of an adept but in the experiential nexus of each moment.

The initiation of the Queen's Chamber has to do with the abandoning of self to such desire to know the Creator in full that the purified instreaming light is drawn in balanced fashion through all energy centers, meeting in indigo and opening the gate to intelligent infinity. Thus the entity experiences true life or, as your people call it, resurrection.

QUESTIONER: You also mentioned that the pyramid was used for learning. Was this the same process or is there a difference?

RA: I am Ra. There is a difference.

QUESTIONER: What is the difference?

RA: I am Ra. The difference is the presence of other-selves manifesting in space/time and after some study, in time/space, for the purpose of teach/learning. In the system created by us, schools were apart from the pyramid, the experiences being solitary.

QUESTIONER: I didn't quite understand what you meant by that. Could you tell me more of what you are talking about?

RA: I am Ra. This is a wide subject. Please restate for specificity.

QUESTIONER: Did you mean that teachers from your vibration or density were manifest in the Queen's Chamber to teach those initiates, or did you mean something else?

RA: I am Ra. In our system, experiences in the Queen's Chamber position were solitary. In Atlantis and in South America, teachers shared the pyramid experiences.

QUESTIONER: How did this learning process take place—learning or teaching—in the pyramid?

RA: I am Ra. How does teach/learning and learn/teaching ever take place?

QUESTIONER: The dangerous pyramid shape for use today would be a four-sided pyramid that was large enough to create the King's Chamber effect. Is that statement correct?

RA: I am Ra. This statement is correct with the additional understanding that the 76° apex angle is that characteristic of the powerful shape.

QUESTIONER: Then I am assuming that we should not use a pyramid of 76° at the apex angle under any circumstances. Is that correct?

RA: I am Ra. This is at your discretion.

QUESTIONER: I will restate the question. I am assuming then that it might be dangerous to use a 76° angle pyramid, and I will ask what angle less than 76° would be roughly the first angle that would not produce this dangerous effect?

RA: I am Ra. Your assumption is correct. The lesser angle may be any angle less than 70°.

QUESTIONER: Thank you. I want to go on with more questioning on the pyramid, but I want to ask a question that [name] has here. I'll throw it in at this point. Could you please expand on the concept of space/time and time/space and how to get past this concept, and what density level do these concepts no longer affect the individual?

RA: I am Ra. This will be the last full query of this working. This instrument has some vital energy left. However, we become concerned with the increasing distortions of the body complex towards pain.

The space/time and time/space concepts are those concepts describing as mathematically as possible the relationships of your illusion, that which is seen to that which is unseen. These descriptive terms are clumsy. They, however, suffice for this work.

In the experiences of the mystical search for unity, these need never be considered, for they are but part of an illusory system. The seeker seeks the One. The One is to be sought, as we have said, by the balanced and self-accepting self-aware, both of its apparent distortions and its total perfection. Resting in this balanced awareness, the entity then opens the self to the universe which it is. The light energy of all things may then be attracted by this intense seeking, and wherever the inner seeking meets the attracted cosmic prana, realization of the One takes place.

The purpose of clearing each energy center is to allow that meeting place to occur at the indigo-ray vibration, thus making contact with intelligent infinity and dissolving all illusions. Service to others is automatic at the released energy generated by this state of consciousness.

The space/time and time/space distinctions, as you understand them, do not hold sway except in third density. However, fourth, fifth, and, to some extent, sixth work within some system of polarized space/time and time/space.

The calculation necessary to move from one system to another through the dimensions are somewhat difficult. Therefore, we have the most difficulty sharing numerical concepts with you and take this opportunity to repeat our request that you monitor our numbers and query any that seem questionable.

Is there a brief query that we may answer before we leave this instrument?

QUESTIONER: Is there anything that we can do to make the instrument more comfortable or to improve the contact?

RA: I am Ra. All is harmonious. We greet you all in joy. The adjustments are satisfactory.

I am Ra. I leave you in the love and in the light of the One Infinite Creator. Go forth, therefore, rejoicing in the power and in the peace of the One Infinite Creator. Adonai.

Session 58,
June 16, 1981

RA: I am Ra. I greet you in the love and in the light of the One Infinite Creator. We communicate now.

QUESTIONER: Would you please give me an indication of the instrument's condition?

RA: I am Ra. This condition is as previously noted, except that the physical distortions mentioned have somewhat increased.

QUESTIONER: Could you tell me the cause of the increase of the physical distortions.

RA: I am Ra. Physical distortions of this nature are begun, as we have said, due to overactivity of weak, as you call this distortion, portions of the body complex. The worsening is due to the nature of the distortion itself, which you call arthritis. Once begun, the distortion will unpredictably remain and unpredictably worsen or lessen.

QUESTIONER: We have tried healing with the diamond crystal. I have tried both using the crystal around my neck and dangling it from a chain held in my right hand. I think that possibly that to do the best work on the wrist I should dangle the crystal just below my right hand from a distance of just a centimeter or two, holding it directly above the wrist. Is this correct?

RA: I am Ra. This would be appropriate if you were practiced at your healing art. To work with a powerful crystal such as you have, while unable to perceive the magnetic flux of the subtle bodies, is perhaps the same as recommending that the beginner, with saw and nail, create the Vatican.

There is great art in the use of the swung crystal. At this point in your development, you would do well to work with the unpowerful crystals in ascertaining not only the physical major energy centers, but also the physical secondary and tertiary energy centers and then begin to find the corresponding subtle body energy centers. In this way, you may activate your own inner vision.

QUESTIONER: What type of crystal should be used for that?

RA: I am Ra. You may use any dangling weight of symmetrical form, for your purpose is not to disturb or manipulate these energy centers but merely to locate them and become aware of what they feel like when in a balanced state and when in an unbalanced or blocked state.

QUESTIONER: Am I correct in assuming that what I am to do is to dangle a weight approximately 2 feet below my hand and place it over the body, and when the weight starts moving in a clockwise rotational direction, it would indicate an unblocked energy center. Is this correct?

RA: I am Ra. The measurement from hand to weight is unimportant and at your discretion. The circular motion shows an unblocked energy center. However, some entities are polarized the reverse of others, and, therefore, it is well to test the form of normal energy spirals before beginning the procedure.

QUESTIONER: How would you test?

RA: I am Ra. Test is done by first holding the weight over your own hand and observing your particular configuration. Then, using the other-self's hand, repeat the procedure.

QUESTIONER: In the case of the instrument, we are concerned with the healing of the wrists and hands. Would I then test the energy center of the instrument's wrist area? Is this correct?

RA: I am Ra. We have given you general information regarding this form of healing and have explicated the instrument's condition. There is a line beyond which information is an intrusion upon the Law of Confusion.

QUESTIONER: I would like to trace the energy patterns and what is actually happening in these patterns and flow of energy in a couple of instances. I would first take the pyramid shape and trace the energy that is focused somehow by this shape. I will make a statement and let you correct it.
   I think that the pyramid can be in any orientation and provide some focusing of spiraling energy, but the greatest focusing of it occurs when one side of it is precisely parallel to magnetic north. Is this correct?

RA: I am Ra. This is substantially correct with one addition. If one corner is oriented to the magnetic north, the energy will be enhanced in its focus also.

QUESTIONER: Do you mean that if I drew a line through two opposite corners of the pyramid at the base and aimed that at magnetic north—that would be precisely 45° out of the orientation of one side aimed at magnetic north—that it would work just as well? Is that what you are saying?

RA: I am Ra. It would work much better than if the pyramid shape were quite unaligned. It would not work quite as efficiently as the aforementioned configuration.

QUESTIONER: Would the pyramid shape work just as well right side up as upside down with respect to the surface of the Earth, assuming the magnetic alignment was the same in both cases?

RA: I am Ra. We do not penetrate your query. The reversed shape of the pyramid reverses the effects of the pyramid. Further, it is difficult to build such a structure, point down. Perhaps we have misinterpreted your query.

QUESTIONER: I used this question only to understand the way the pyramid focuses light, not for the purpose of using one. I was just saying if we did build a pyramid point down, would it focus at the Queen's Chamber position or just below it the same way as if it were point up?

RA: I am Ra. It would only work thusly if an entity's polarity were, for some reason, reversed.

QUESTIONER: Then the lines of spiraling light energy—do they originate from a position towards the center of the Earth and radiate outward from that point?

RA: I am Ra. The pyramid shape is a collector which draws the instreaming energy from what you would term the bottom or base, and allows this energy to spiral upward in a line with the apex of this shape. This is also true if a pyramid shape is upended. The energy is not Earth energy, as we understand your question, but is light energy, which is omnipresent.

QUESTIONER: Does it matter if the pyramid is solid or is made of four thin sides, or is there a difference in effect between those two makes?

RA: I am Ra. As an energy collector, the shape itself is the only requirement. From the standpoint of the practical needs of your body complexes, if one is to house one's self in such a shape, it is well that this shape be solid sided in order to avoid being inundated by outer stimuli.

QUESTIONER: Then if I just used a wire frame that was four pieces of wire joined at the apex running down to the base, and the pyramid were totally open, this would do the same thing to the spiraling light energy? Is this correct?

RA: I am Ra. The concept of the frame as equal to the solid form is correct. However, there are many metals not recommended for use in pyramid shapes designed to aid the meditative process. Those that are recommended are, in your system of barter, what you call expensive. The wood, or other natural materials, or the man-made plastic rods will also be of service.

QUESTIONER: Why is the spiraling light focused by something as open and simple as four wooden rods joined at an apex angle?

RA: I am Ra. If you pictured light in the metaphysical sense, as water, and the pyramid shape as a funnel, this concept might become self-evident.

QUESTIONER: Thank you. I do not wish to get into subject matter of no importance. I had assumed that questions about the pyramid were desired by you due to the fact that some danger was involved to some who had misused the pyramid, etc.

I am trying to understand the way light works and am trying to get a grasp of how everything works together, and I was hoping that questions on the pyramid would help me understand the third distortion, which is light. As I understand it, the pyramid shape acts as a funnel increasing the density of energy so that the individual may have a greater intensity of actually the third distortion. Is this correct?

RA: I am Ra. In general, this is correct.

QUESTIONER: Then the pure crystalline shape, such as the diamond, you mentioned as being frozen light—it seems that this third-density physical manifestation of light is somehow a window or focusing mechanism for the third distortion in a general sense. Is this correct?

RA: I am Ra. This is basically correct. However, it may be noted that only the will of the crystallized entity may cause interdimensional light to flow through this material. The more regularized the entity, and the more regularized the crystal, the more profound the effect.

QUESTIONER: There are many people who are now bending metal, doing other things like that by mentally requesting this happen. What is happening in that case?

RA: I am Ra. That which occurs in this instance may be likened to the influence of the second spiral of light in a pyramid being used by an entity. As this second spiral ends at the apex, the light may be likened unto a laser beam in the metaphysical sense and when intelligently directed may cause bending not only in the pyramid, but this is the type of energy which is tapped into by those capable of this focusing of the upward-spiraling light. This is made possible through contact in indigo ray with intelligent energy.

QUESTIONER: Why are these people able to do this? They seem to have no training; they are just able to do it.

RA: I am Ra. They remember the disciplines necessary for this activity, which is merely useful upon other true color vibratory experiential nexi.

QUESTIONER: Then you are saying that this wouldn't be useful in our present density. Will it be useful in fourth density on this planet in the very near future?

RA: I am Ra. The end of such energy focusing is to build, not to destroy, and it does become quite useful as, shall we say, an alternative to third-density building methods.

QUESTIONER: Is it also used for healing?

RA: I am Ra. No.

QUESTIONER: Is there any advantage in attempting to develop these characteristics or in being able to bend metal, etc.? What I am trying to say is, are these characteristics a signpost of the development of an entity, or is it merely something else? For instance, as an entity develops through his indigo, would a signpost of his development be this bending ability?

RA: I am Ra. This will be the last full query of this working.

Let us specify the three spirals of light energy which the pyramid exemplifies. Firstly, the fundamental spiral, which is used for study and for healing. Second, the spiral to the apex, which is used for building. Thirdly, the spiral spreading from the apex, which is used for energizing.

Contact with indigo ray need not necessarily show itself in any certain gift or guidepost, as you have said. There are some whose indigo energy is that of pure being and never is manifested, yet all are aware of such an entity's progress. Others may teach or share in many ways contact with intelligent energy. Others continue in unmanifested form, seeking intelligent infinity.

Thus the manifestation is lesser signpost than that which is sensed or intuited about a mind/body/spirit complex. This violet-ray beingness is far more indicative of true self.

Are there any brief queries or small matters we may clear up, if we can, before we leave this instrument?

QUESTIONER: I did have a question on what you meant by the "third spiral," and if that is too long I would just ask if there is anything that we can do to make the instrument more comfortable or to improve the contact?

RA: I am Ra. We may answer briefly. You may query in more detail if you deem it desirable at another session.

If you picture the candle flame, you may see the third spiral. This instrument is well balanced. The accoutrements are aligned well. You are conscientious.

I am Ra. I leave you, my friends, in the love and in the light of the One Infinite Creator. Go forth, therefore, rejoicing in the power and the peace of the One Infinite Creator. Adonai.

Session 59,
June 25, 1981

RA: I am Ra. I greet you in the love and in the light of the One Infinite Creator. We communicate now.

QUESTIONER: Could you first tell me the instrument's condition and why she feels so tired?

RA: I am Ra. This instrument's condition is as previously stated. We cannot infringe upon your free will by discussing the latter query.

QUESTIONER: Would it be any greater protection for the instrument if [name] changed his sitting position to the other side of the bed?

RA: I am Ra. No.

QUESTIONER: At the end of the second major cycle, there were a few hundred thousand people on Earth. There are over four billion people on Earth today. Were the over four billion people that are incarnate today in the Earth planes and not incarnate at that time, or did they come in from elsewhere during the last 25,000 years?

RA: I am Ra. There were three basic divisions of origin of these entities.

Firstly, and primarily, those of the planetary sphere you call Maldek, having become able to take up third density once again, were gradually loosed from self-imposed limitations of form.

Secondly, there were those of other third-density entrance or neophytes whose vibratory patterns matched the Terran experiential nexus. These then filtered in through incarnative processes.

Thirdly, in the past approximate 200 of your years you have experienced much visiting of the Wanderers. It may be noted that all possible opportunities for incarnation are being taken at this time due to your harvesting process and the opportunities which this offers.

QUESTIONER: Just to clarify that, could you tell me approximately how many mind/body/spirit complexes were transferred to Earth at the beginning of this last 75,000-year period?

RA: I am Ra. The transfer, as you call it, has been gradual. Over two billion souls are those of Maldek which have successfully made the transition.

Approximately 1.9 billion souls have, from many portions of the creation, entered into this experience at various times. The remainder are those who have experienced the first two cycles upon this sphere or who have come in at some point as Wanderers; some Wanderers having been in this sphere for many thousands of your years; others having come far more recently.

QUESTIONER: I'm trying to understand the three spirals of light in the pyramid shape. I would like to question on each.

The first spiral starts below the Queen's Chamber and ends in the Queen's Chamber? Is that correct?

RA: I am Ra. This is incorrect. The first notion of upward-spiraling light is as that of the scoop, the light energy being scooped in through the attraction of the pyramid shape through the bottom or base. Thus the first configuration is a semi-spiral.

QUESTIONER: Would this be similar to the vortex you get when you release water from a bathtub?

RA: I am Ra. This is correct except that in the case of this action, the cause is gravitic, whereas in the case of the pyramid, the vortex is that of upward-spiraling light being attracted by the electromagnetic fields engendered by the shape of the pyramid.

QUESTIONER: Then the first spiral after this semispiral is the spiral used for study and healing. Relative to the Queen's Chamber position, where does this first spiral begin and end?

RA: I am Ra. The spiral which is used for study and healing begins at or slightly below the Queen's Chamber position, depending upon your Earth and cosmic rhythms. It moves through the King's Chamber position in a sharply delineated form and ends at the point whereby the top approximate third of the pyramid may be seen to be intensifying the energy.

QUESTIONER: The first spiral is obviously different somehow from the second and third spirals, since they have different uses and different properties. The second spiral then starts at the end of the first spiral and goes up to the apex. Is that correct?

RA: I am Ra. This is partially correct. The large spiral is drawn into the vortex of the apex of the pyramid. However, some light energy which is of the more intense nature of the red, shall we say, end of the spectrum is spiraled once again, causing an enormous strengthening and focusing of energy which is then of use for building.

QUESTIONER: And then the third spiral radiates from the top of the pyramid. Is this correct?

RA: I am Ra. The third complete spiral does so. This is correct. It is well to reckon with the foundation semi-spiral which supplies the prana for all that may be affected by the three following upward spirals of light.

QUESTIONER: Now I am trying to understand what happens in this process. I'll call the first semi-spiral zero position, and the other three spirals 1, 2, and 3, the first spiral being a study in healing. What change takes place in light from zero position to the first spiral that makes that first spiral available for healing?

RA: I am Ra. The prana scooped in by the pyramid shape gains coherence of energetic direction. The term "upward-spiraling light" is an indication not of your up-and-down concept, but an indication of the concept of that which reaches towards the source of love and light.

Thus, all light or prana is upward spiraling, but its direction, as you understand this term, is unregimented and not useful for work.

QUESTIONER: Could I assume then that from all points in space, light radiates in our illusion outward in a 360° solid angle, and this scoop shape with the pyramid then creates the coherence to this radiation as a focusing mechanism? Is this correct?

RA: I am Ra. This is precisely correct.

QUESTIONER: Then the first spiral has a different factor of cohesion, you might say, than the second. What is the difference between this first and second spiral?

RA: I am Ra. As the light is funneled into what you term the zero position, it reaches the point of turning. This acts as a compression of the light, multiplying tremendously its coherence and organization.

QUESTIONER: Then is the coherence and organization multiplied once more at the start of the second spiral? Is there just a doubling effect or an increasing effect?

RA: I am Ra. This is difficult to discuss in your language. There is no doubling effect but a transformation across boundaries of dimension, so that light which was working for those using it in space/time-time/space configuration becomes light working in what you might consider an interdimensional time/space-space/time configuration. This causes an apparent diffusion and weakness of the spiraling energy. However, in position 2, as you have called it, much work may be done interdimensionally.

QUESTIONER: In the Giza pyramid there was no chamber at position 2. Do you ever make use of position 2 by putting a chamber in that position on other planets or in other pyramids?

RA: I am Ra. This position is useful only to those whose abilities are such that they are capable of serving as conductors of this type of focused spiral. One would not wish to attempt to train third-density entities in such disciplines.

QUESTIONER: Then the third spiral radiating from the top of the pyramid you say is used for energizing. Can you tell me what you mean by "energizing"?

RA: I am Ra. The third spiral is extremely full of the positive effects of directed prana, and that which is placed over such a shape will receive shocks energizing the electromagnetic fields. This can be most stimulating in third-density applications of mental and bodily configurations. However, if allowed to be in place overlong, such shocks may traumatize the entity.

QUESTIONER: Are there any other effects of the pyramid shape beside the spirals that we have just discussed?

RA: I am Ra. There are several. However, their uses are limited. The use of the resonating chamber position is one which challenges the ability of an adept to face the self. This is one type of mental test which may be used. It is powerful and quite dangerous.

The outer shell of the pyramid shape contains small vortices of light energy which, in the hands of capable crystallized beings, are useful for various subtle workings upon the healing of invisible bodies affecting the physical body.

Other of these places are those wherein perfect sleep may be obtained and age reversed. These characteristics are not important.

QUESTIONER: What position would be the age reversal position?

RA: I am Ra. Approximately 5° to 10° above and below the Queen's Chamber position in ovoid shapes on each face of the four-sided pyramid, extending into the solid shape approximately one-quarter of the way to the Queen's Chamber position.

QUESTIONER: In other words, if I went just inside the wall of the pyramid a quarter of the way but still remained three-quarters of the way from the center at approximately the level above the base of the Queen's Chamber, I would find that position?

RA: I am Ra. This is approximately so. You must picture the double teardrop extending in both the plane of the pyramid face and in half towards the Queen's Chamber, extending above and below it. You may see this as the position where the light has been scooped into the spiral and then is expanding again. This position is what you may call a prana vacuum.

QUESTIONER: Why would this reverse aging?

RA: I am Ra. Aging is a function of the effects of various electromagnetic fields upon the electromagnetic fields of the mind/body/spirit complex. In this position there is no input or disturbance of the fields, nor is any activity within the electromagnetic field complex of the mind/body/spirit complex allowed full sway. The vacuum sucks any such disturbance away. Thus the entity feels nothing and is suspended.

QUESTIONER: Is the pyramid shape constructed in our yard functioning properly? Is it aligned properly and built properly?

RA: I am Ra. It is built within good tolerances, though not perfect. However, its alignment should be as this resting place for maximum efficacy.

QUESTIONER: Do you mean that one of the base sides should be aligned 20° east of north?

RA: I am Ra. That alignment would be efficacious.

QUESTIONER: Previously you stated that one of the base sides should be aligned with magnetic north. Which is better, to align with magnetic north or to align with 20° east of magnetic north?

RA: I am Ra. This is at your discretion. The proper alignment for you of this sphere at this time is magnetic north. However, in your query you asked specifically about a structure which has been used by specific entities whose energy vortices are more consonant with the, shall we say, true color green orientation. This would be the 20° east of north.

There are advantages to each orientation. The effect is stronger at magnetic north and can be felt more clearly. The energy, though weak, coming from the now-distant but soon to be paramount direction is more helpful.

The choice is yours. It is the choice between quantity and quality or wide-band and narrow-band aid in meditation.

QUESTIONER: When the planetary axis realigns, will it realign 20° east of north to conform to the green vibration?

RA: I am Ra. We fear this shall be the last question, as this entity rapidly increases its distortion towards what you call pain of the body complex.

There is every indication that this will occur. We cannot speak of certainties but are aware that the grosser or less dense materials will be pulled into conformation with the denser and lighter energies which give your Logos its proceedings through the realms of experience.

May we answer any brief queries at this time?

QUESTIONER: Only if there is anything that we can do to make the instrument more comfortable or to improve the contact?

RA: I am Ra. All is well. We are aware that you experience difficulties at this time, but they are not due to your lack of conscientiousness or dedication. I am Ra. I leave you in the love and in the light of the One Infinite Creator. Go forth, then, rejoicing in the power and the peace of the One Infinite Creator. Adonai.

Session 60,
July 1, 1981

RA: I am Ra. I greet you in the love and in the light of the One Infinite Creator. We communicate now.

QUESTIONER: When you spoke in the last session of "energizing shocks" coming from the top of the pyramid, did you mean that these came at intervals rather than steadily?

RA: I am Ra. These energizing shocks come at discrete intervals but come very, very close together in a properly functioning pyramid shape. In one whose dimensions have gone awry, the energy will not be released with regularity or in quanta, as you may perhaps better understand our meaning.

QUESTIONER: The next statement that I will make may or may not be enlightening to me in my investigation of the pyramid energy, but it has occurred to me that the effect of the so-called Bermuda Triangle could be possibly due to a large pyramid beneath the water which releases this third spiral in discrete and varying intervals. Entities or craft that are in the vicinity may change their space/time continuum in some way. Is this correct?

RA: I am Ra. Yes.

QUESTIONER: Then this third spiral has an energizing effect that, if strong enough, will actually change the space/time continuum. Is there a use or value to this type of change?

RA: I am Ra. In the hands of one of fifth density or above, this particular energy may be tapped in order to communicate information, love, or light across what you would consider vast distances, but which with this energy may be considered transdimensional leaps. Also, there is the possibility of travel using this formation of energy.

QUESTIONER: Would this travel be the instantaneous type used primarily by sixth-density entities, or is it the slingshot effect that you are talking about?

RA: I am Ra. The former effect is that of which we speak. You may note that as one learns the, shall we say, understandings or disciplines of the personality, each of these configurations of prana is available to the entity without the aid of this shape. One may view the pyramid at Giza as metaphysical training wheels.

QUESTIONER: Then is the large underwater pyramid off the Florida coast one of the balancing pyramids that Ra constructed, or did some other social memory complex construct it, and, if so, which one?

RA: I am Ra. That pyramid of which you speak was one whose construction was aided by sixth-density entities of a social memory complex working with Atlanteans prior to our working with the, as you call them, Egyptians.

QUESTIONER: You mentioned working with one other group other than the Egyptians. Who were they?

RA: I am Ra. These entities were those of South America. We divided our forces to work within these two cultures.

QUESTIONER: The pyramid shape then, as I understand it, was deemed by your social memory complex to be at that time of paramount importance as the physical-training aid for spiritual development. At this particular time in the evolution of our planet, it seems that you place little or no emphasis on this shape. Is this correct?

RA: I am Ra. This is correct. It is our honor/duty to attempt to remove the distortions that the use of this shape has caused in the thinking of your peoples and in the activities of some of your entities. We do not deny that such shapes are efficacious, nor do we withhold the general gist of this efficacy. However, we wish to offer our understanding, limited though it is, that contrary to our naive beliefs many thousands of your years ago, the optimum shape for initiation does not exist.

Let us expand upon this point. When we were aided by sixth-density entities during our own third-density experiences, we, being less bellicose in the extreme, found this teaching to be of help. In our naiveté in third density, we had not developed the interrelationships of your barter or money system and power. We were, in fact, a more philosophical third-density planet than your own, and our choices of polarity were much more centered about the, shall we say, understanding of sexual energy transfers and the appropriate relationships between self and other-self.

We spent a much larger portion of our space/time working with the unmanifested being. In this less complex atmosphere, it was quite instructive to have this learn/teaching device, and we benefited without the distortions we found occurring among your peoples.

We have recorded these differences meticulously in the Great Record of Creation that such naiveté shall not be necessary again.

At this space/time we may best serve you, we believe, by stating that the pyramid for meditation along with other rounded and arched or pointed circular shapes is of help to you. However, it is our observation that due to the complexity of influences upon the unmanifested being at this space/time nexus among your planetary peoples, it is best that the progress of the mind/body/spirit complex take place without, as you call them, training aids, because when using a training aid, an entity then takes upon itself the Law of Responsibility for the quickened or increased rate of learn/teaching. If this greater understanding, if we may use this misnomer, is not put into practice in the moment-by-moment experience of the entity, then the usefulness of the training aid becomes negative.

QUESTIONER: Thank you. I don't know if this question will result in any useful information, but I feel that I must ask it. What was the Ark of the Covenant, and what was its use?

RA: I am Ra. The Ark of the Covenant was that place wherein those things most holy, according to the understanding of the one called Moishe, were placed. The article placed therein has been called by your peoples two tablets called the Ten Commandments. There were not two tablets. There was one writing in scroll. This was placed along with the most carefully written accounts by various entities of their beliefs concerning the creation by the One Creator.

This ark was designed to constitute the place wherefrom the priests, as you call those distorted towards the desire to serve their brothers, could draw their power and feel the presence of the One Creator. However, it is to be noted that this entire arrangement was designed not by the one known to the Confederation as Yahweh but rather was designed by negative entities preferring this method of creating an elite called the Sons of Levi.

QUESTIONER: Was this a device for communication then? You also said that they drew power from it. What sort of power? How did this work?

RA: I am Ra. This was charged by means of the materials with which it was built, being given an electromagnetic field. It became an object of power in this way, and, to those whose faith became that untarnished by unrighteousness or separation, this power designed for negativity became positive and is so, to those truly in harmony with the experience of service, to this day. Thus the negative forces were partially successful, but the positively oriented Moishe, as this entity was called, gave to your planetary peoples the possibility of a path to the One Infinite Creator which is completely positive.

This is in common with each of your orthodox religious systems, which have all become somewhat mixed in orientation yet offer a pure path to the One Creator which is seen by the pure seeker.

QUESTIONER: Where is the Ark of the Covenant now? Where is it located?

RA: I am Ra. We refrain from answering this query due to the fact that it does still exist and is not that which we would infringe upon your peoples by locating.

QUESTIONER: In trying to understand the creative energies, it has occurred to me that I really do not understand why unusable heat is generated as our Earth moves from third into fourth density. I know it has to do with disharmony between the vibrations of third and fourth density, but why this would show up as a physical heating within the Earth is beyond me. Can you enlighten me on that?

RA: I am Ra. The concepts are somewhat difficult to penetrate in your language. However, we shall attempt to speak to the subject. If an entity is not in harmony with its circumstances, it feels a burning within. The temperature of the physical vehicle does not yet rise, only the heat of the temper or the tears, as we may describe this disharmony. However, if an entity persists for a long period of your space/time in feeling this emotive heat and disharmony, the entire body complex will begin to resonate to this disharmony, and the disharmony will then show up as the cancer or other degenerative distortions from what you call health.

When an entire planetary system of peoples and cultures repeatedly experiences disharmony on a great scale, the earth under the feet of these entities shall begin to resonate with this disharmony. Due to the nature of the physical vehicle, disharmony shows up as a blockage of growth or an uncontrolled growth, since the primary function of a mind/body/spirit complex's bodily complex is growth and maintenance. In the case of your planet, the purpose of the planet is the maintenance of orbit and the proper location or orientation with regards to other cosmic influences. In order to have this occurring properly, the interior of your sphere is hot in your physical terms. Thus instead of uncontrolled growth you begin to experience uncontrolled heat and its expansive consequences.

QUESTIONER: Is the Earth solid all the way through from one side to the other?

RA: I am Ra. You may say that your sphere is of an honeycomb nature. The center is, however, solid if you would so call that which is molten.

QUESTIONER: Are there third-density entities living in the honeycomb areas? Is this correct?

RA: I am Ra. This was at one time correct. This is not correct at this present space/time.

QUESTIONER: Are there any inner civilizations or entities living in these areas other than physically incarnate who do come and materialize on the Earth's surface at some times?

RA: I am Ra. As we have noted, there are some which do as you say. Further, there are some inner-plane entities of this planet which prefer to do some materialization into third density visible in these areas. There are also bases, shall we say, in these areas of those from elsewhere, both positive and negative. There are abandoned cities.

QUESTIONER: What are these bases used for by those from elsewhere?

RA: I am Ra. These bases are used for the work of materialization of needed equipment for communication with third-density entities and for resting places for some equipment which you might call small craft. These are used for surveillance when it is requested by entities.

Thus some of the, shall we say, teachers of the Confederation speak partially through these surveillance instruments along computerized lines, and when information is desired and those requesting it are of the proper vibratory level, the Confederation entity itself will then speak.

QUESTIONER: I understand then that the Confederation entity needs communication equipment and craft to communicate with the third-density incarnate entity requesting the information?

RA: I am Ra. This is incorrect. However, many of your peoples request the same basic information in enormous repetition, and for a social memory complex to speak ad infinitum about the need to meditate is a waste of the considerable abilities of such social memory complexes.

Thus some entities have had approved by the Council of Saturn the placement and maintenance of these message givers for those whose needs are simple, thus reserving the abilities of the Confederation members for those already meditating and absorbing information which are then ready for additional information.

QUESTIONER: There has been, for the past thirty years, a lot of information and a lot of confusion, and in fact, I would say that the Law of Confusion has been working overtime—to make a small joke—in bringing information for spiritual catalysis to groups requesting it, and we know that both the positively and the negatively oriented social memory complexes have been adding to this information as they can. This has led to a condition of apathy in a lot of cases with respect to the information. Many who are truly seeking have been thwarted by what I might call spiritual entropy in this information. Can you comment on this and the mechanisms of alleviating these problems?

RA: I am Ra. We can comment on this.

QUESTIONER: Only if you deem it of importance would I request a comment.
    If you deem it of no importance, we'll skip it.

RA: I am Ra. This information is significant to some degree, as it bears upon our own mission at this time.
    We of the Confederation are at the call of those upon your planet. If the call, though sincere, is fairly low in consciousness of the, shall we say, system whereby spiritual evolution may be precipitated, then we may only offer that information useful to that particular caller. This is the basic difficulty. Entities receive the basic information about the Original Thought and the means—that is, meditation and service to others—whereby this Original Thought may be obtained.
    Please note that as Confederation members we are speaking for positively oriented entities. We believe the Orion group has precisely the same difficulty.
    Once this basic information is received, it is not put into practice in the heart and in the life experience but instead rattles about within the mind complex distortions as would a building block which has lost its place and simply rolls from side to side uselessly, yet still the entity calls. Therefore, the same basic information is repeated. Ultimately the entity decides that it is weary of this repetitive information. However, if an entity puts into practice that which it is given, it will not find repetition except when needed.

QUESTIONER: Thank you. Are the chakras or bodily energy centers related to or do they operate like the pyramid energy funnel?

RA: I am Ra. No.

QUESTIONER: Was there a purpose for mummification having to do with anything other than bodily burial?

RA: I am Ra. Much as we would like to speak to you of this distortion of our designs in constructing the pyramid, we can say very little, for the intent was quite mixed and the uses, though many felt them to be positive, were of a nonpositive order of generation. We cannot speak upon this subject without infringement upon some basic energy balances between the positive and negative forces upon your planet. It may be said that those offering themselves felt they were offering themselves in service to others.

QUESTIONER: What civilization was it that helped Ra using the pyramid shape while Ra was in third density?

RA: I am Ra. Your people have a fondness for the naming. These entities have begun their travel back to the Creator and are no longer experiencing time.

QUESTIONER: The instrument wished to know, when using the pendulum in discovering energy centers, what the back-and-forth motion meant instead of the circular motion?

RA: I am Ra. This shall have to be the final question, although this entity is still providing us with energy. It is experiencing the distortion towards pain.

The rotations having been discussed, we shall simply say that the weak back-and-forth motion indicates a partial blockage, although not a complete blockage. The strong back-and-forth motion indicates the reverse of blockage, which is over-stimulation of a chakra or energy center, which is occurring in order to attempt to balance some difficulty in body or mind complex activity. This condition is not helpful to the entity, as it is unbalanced. Are there any brief queries before we leave this instrument?

QUESTIONER: Only is there anything that we can do to make the instrument more comfortable or to improve the contact?

RA: I am Ra. Be merry, my friends. All is well and your conscientiousness is to be recommended. We leave you in the love and the light of the One Infinite Creator. Rejoice, then, and go forth in the peace and in the glory of the One Infinite Creator. I am Ra. Adonai.

Session 61,
July 8, 1981

RA: I am Ra. I greet you, my friends, in the love and in the light of the Infinite Creator. We communicate now.

QUESTIONER: Could you give me an indication of the instrument's condition?

RA: I am Ra. This instrument's vital energies are improving. The physical complex distortions are quite marked at this space/time, and there is a decrease in physical complex energies.

QUESTIONER: Is there anything in particular that the instrument could do to improve the physical condition?

RA: I am Ra. This instrument has two factors affecting its bodily distortions. This is in common with all those which by seniority of vibration have reached the green-ray level of vibratory consciousness complexes.

The first is the given instreamings, which vary from cycle to cycle in predictable manner. In this particular entity the cyclical complexes at this space/time nexus are not favorable for the physical energy levels.

The second ramification of condition is that which we might call the degree of mental efficiency in use of catalyst provided for the learning of programmed lessons in particular and the lessons of love in general.

This instrument, unlike some entities, has some further distortion due to the use of pre-incarnative conditions.

QUESTIONER: Can you expand on what you meant by the "cycling instreamings of energy"?

RA: I am Ra. There are four types of cycles which are those given in the moment of entry into incarnation. There are in addition more cosmic and less regularized inpourings which, from time to time, affect a sensitized mind/body/spirit complex. The four rhythms are, to some extent, known among your peoples and are called biorhythms.

There is a fourth cycle which we may call the cycle of gateway of magic of the adept or of the spirit. This is a cycle which is completed in approximately eighteen of your diurnal cycles.

The cosmic patterns are also a function of the moment of incarnative entrance and have to do with your satellite you call the moon, your planets of this galaxy, the galactic sun, and in some cases the instreamings from the major galactic points of energy flow.

QUESTIONER: Would it be helpful to plot these cycles for the instrument and attempt to have these sessions at the most favorable points with respect to the cycles?

RA: I am Ra. To that specific query we have no response.

It may be noted that the three in this triad bring in this energy pattern which is Ra. Thus each energy input of the triad is of note.

We may say that while these information systems are interesting, they are in sway only insofar as the entity or entities involved have not made totally efficient use of catalyst, and, therefore, instead of accepting the, shall we say, negative or retrograde moments or periods without undue notice, have the distortion towards the retaining of these distortions in order to work out the unused catalyst.

It is to be noted that psychic attack continues upon this entity, although it is only effective at this time in physical distortions towards discomfort.

We may suggest that it is always of some interest to observe the roadmap, both of the cycles and of the planetary and other cosmic influences, in that one may see certain wide roads or possibilities. However, we remind that this group is an unit.

QUESTIONER: Is there some way that we could, as a unit, then, do something to reduce the effect of the psychic attack on the instrument and optimize the communicative opportunity?

RA: I am Ra. We have given you the information concerning that which aids this particular mind/body/spirit complex. We can speak no further. It is our opinion, which we humbly offer, that each is in remarkable harmony with each for this particular third-density illusion at this space/time nexus.

QUESTIONER: I would like to ask questions about healing exercises. The first is, in the healing exercises concerning the body, what do you mean by the disciplines of the body having to do with the balance between love and wisdom in the use of the body in its natural functions?

RA: I am Ra. We shall speak more briefly than usual due to this instrument's use of the transferred energy. We, therefore, request further queries if our reply is not sufficient.

The body complex has natural functions. Many of these have to do with the unmanifested self and are normally not subject to the need for balancing. There are natural functions which have to do with other-self. Among these are touching, loving, the sexual life, and those times when the company of another is craved to combat the type of loneliness which is the natural function of the body, as opposed to those types of loneliness which are of the mind/emotion complex or of the spirit.

When these natural functions may be observed in the daily life, they may be examined in order that the love of self and love of other-self versus the wisdom regarding the use of natural functions may be observed. There are many fantasies and stray thoughts which may be examined in most of your peoples in this balancing process.

Equally to be balanced is the withdrawal from the need for these natural functions with regard to other-self. On the one hand there is an excess of love. It must be determined whether this is love of self or other-self or both. On the other hand there is an overbalance towards wisdom.

It is well to know the body complex so that it is an ally, balanced and ready to be clearly used as a tool, for each bodily function may be used in higher and higher, if you will, complexes of energy with other-self. No matter what the behavior, the important balancing is the understanding of each interaction on this level with other-selves, so that whether the balance may be love/wisdom or wisdom/love, the other-self is seen by the self in a balanced configuration, and the self is thus freed for further work.

QUESTIONER: Then the second question is, could you give an example of how feelings affect portions of the body and the sensations of the body?

RA: I am Ra. It is nearly impossible to speak generally of these mechanisms, for each entity of proper seniority has its own programming. Of the less aware entities we may say that the connection will often seem random, as the Higher Self continues producing catalyst until a bias occurs. In each programmed individual the sensitivities are far more active, and, as we have said, that catalyst not used fully by the mind and spirit is given to the body.

Thus you may see in this entity the numbing of the arms and the hands, signifying this entity's failure to surrender to the loss of control over the life. Thus this drama is enacted in the physical distortion complex.

In the questioner we may see the desire not to be carrying the load it carries given as physical manifestation of the soreness of those muscles for carrying used. That which is truly needed to be carried is a pre-incarnative responsibility, which seems highly inconvenient.

In the case of the scribe we see a weariness and numbness of feelings ensuing from lack of using catalyst designed to sensitize this entity to quite significant influxes of unfamiliar distortion complexes of the mental, emotional, and spiritual level. As the numbness removes itself from the higher or more responsive complexes, the bodily complex distortions will vanish. This is true also of the other examples.

We would note at this time that the totally efficient use of catalyst upon your plane is extremely rare.

QUESTIONER: Could you tell me how you are able to give us information like this with respect to the first distortion or Law of Confusion?

RA: I am Ra. Each of those is already aware of this information. Any other reader may extract the heart of meaning from this discussion without interest as to the examples' sources. If each was not fully aware of these answers, we could not speak.

It is interesting that in many of your queries you ask for confirmation rather than information. This is acceptable to us.

QUESTIONER: This brings out the point of the purpose of the physical incarnation, I believe. And that is to reach a conviction through your own thought processes as to a solution to problems and understandings in a totally free situation with no proof at all or anything that you would consider proof, proof being a very poor word in itself. Can you expand on my concept?

RA: I am Ra. Your opinion is an eloquent one, although somewhat confused in its connections between the freedom expressed by subjective knowing and the freedom expressed by subjective acceptance. There is a significant distinction between the two.

This is not a dimension of knowing, even subjectively, due to the lack of overview of cosmic and other inpourings which affect each and every situation which produces catalyst. The subjective acceptance of that which is at the moment and the finding of love within that moment is the greater freedom.

That known as the subjective knowing without proof is, in some degree, a poor friend, for there will be anomalies no matter how much information is garnered due to the distortions which form third density.

QUESTIONER: The third question that I have here is, could you give examples of bodily polarity?

RA: I am Ra. Within the body there are many polarities which relate to the balancing of the energy centers of the various bodies of the unmanifested entity. It is well to explore these polarities for work in healing.

Each entity is, of course, a potential polarized portion of an other-self.

QUESTIONER: The last question here says that it would seem the proper balancing exercises for all the sensations of the body would be some sort of inactivity such as meditation or contemplation. Is this correct?

RA: I am Ra. This is largely incorrect. The balancing requires a meditative state in order for the work to be done. However, the balancing of sensation has to do with an analysis of the sensation with especial respect to any unbalanced leaning between the love and the wisdom or the positive and the negative. Then whatever is lacking in the balanced sensation is, as in all balancing, allowed to come into the being after the sensation is remembered and recalled in such detail as to overwhelm the senses.

QUESTIONER: Could you tell me why it is important for the appurtenances and other things to be so carefully aligned with respect to the instrument, and why just a small ruffle in the sheet by the instrument causes a problem with the reception of Ra?

RA: I am Ra. We may attempt an explanation. This contact is narrow band. The instrument is highly sensitive. Thus we have good entry into it and can use it to an increasingly satisfactory level.

However, the trance condition is, shall we say, not one which is without toll upon this instrument. Therefore, the area above the entrance into the physical complex of this instrument must be kept clear to avoid discomfort to the instrument, especially as it reenters the body complex. The appurtenances give to the instrument's sensory input mental visualizations which aid in the trance beginning. The careful alignment of these is important for the energizing group in that it is a reminder to that support group that it is time for a working. The ritualistic behaviors are triggers for many energies of the support group. You may have noticed more energy being used in workings as the number has increased due to the long-term, shall we say, effect of such ritualistic actions.

This would not aid another group, as it was designed for this particular system of mind/body/spirit complexes and especially the instrument.

There is enough energy transferred for one more long query. We do not wish to deplete this instrument.

QUESTIONER: Then I will ask this question. Could you tell us the purpose of the frontal lobes of the brain and the conditions necessary for their activation?

RA: I am Ra. The frontal lobes of the brain will, shall we say, have much more use in fourth density.

The primary mental/emotive condition of this large area of the so-called brain is joy or love in its creative sense. Thus the energies which we have discussed in relationship to the pyramids: all of the healing, the learning, the building, and the energizing are to be found in this area. This is the area tapped by the adept. This is the area which, working through the trunk and root of mind, makes contact with intelligent energy and, through this gateway, intelligent infinity.

Are there any queries before we leave this instrument?

QUESTIONER: Only is there anything that we can do to make the instrument more comfortable or to improve the contact?

RA: I am Ra. This instrument is somewhat distorted but each is doing well. You are conscientious. We thank you for continuing to observe the alignments and request that on each level you continue to be this fastidious, as this will maintain the contact.

I am Ra. I leave you in the love and the light of the One Infinite Creator. Go forth, my friends, rejoicing in the power and the peace of the One Infinite Creator. Adonai.

Session 62,
July 13, 1981

RA: I am Ra. I greet you in the love and in the light of the One Infinite Creator.

Before we begin, may we request that a circle be walked about this instrument and that then each of the supporting group expel breath forcibly, approximately two and one-half feet above the instrument's head, the circle then again being walked about the instrument.

[This was done as directed.]

RA: I am Ra. We appreciate your kind cooperation. Please recheck the alignment of perpendicularity and we will begin.

[This was done as directed.]

RA: I am Ra. We communicate now.

QUESTIONER: Could you tell me what was wrong or what caused the necessity for the rewalking of the circle and the purpose for the expelling of the breath?

RA: I am Ra. This instrument was under specific psychic attack at the time of the beginning of the working. There was a slight irregularity in the words verbalized by your sound complex vibratory mechanisms in the protective walking of the circle. Into this opening came this entity and began to work upon the instrument now in trance state, as you would call it. This instrument was being quite adversely affected in physical complex distortions.

Thus the circle was properly walked. The breath of righteousness expelled the thought-form, and the circle again was walked.

QUESTIONER: What was the nature of the thought-form or its affiliation?

RA: I am Ra. This thought-form was of Orion affiliation.

QUESTIONER: Was the attack successful in creating any further distortion in the instrument's physical complex?

RA: I am Ra. This is correct.

QUESTIONER: What is the nature of this distortion?

RA: This thought-form sought to put an end to this instrument's incarnation by working with the renal distortions which, although corrected upon time/space, are vulnerable to one which knows the way to separate time/space molding and space/time distortions which are being unmolded, vulnerable as before the, shall we say, healing.

QUESTIONER: What detrimental effect has been done?

RA: I am Ra. There will be some discomfort. However, we were fortunate in that this instrument was very open to us and well tuned. Had we not been able to reach this instrument and instruct you, the instrument's physical vehicle would soon be unviable.

QUESTIONER: Will there be any lasting effect from this attack as far as the instrument's physical vehicle is concerned?

RA: I am Ra. This is difficult to say. We are of the opinion that no lasting harm or distortion will occur.

The healer was strong and the bonds taking effect in the remolding of these renal distortions were effective. It is at this point a question of two forms of the leavings of what you may call a spell or a magic working; the healer's distortions versus the attempt at Orion distortions; the healer's distortions full of love; the Orion distortions also pure in separation. It seems that all is well except for some possible discomfort which shall be attended if persistent.

QUESTIONER: Was the opening that was made in the protective circle planned to be made by the Orion entity? Was it a specific planned attempt to make an opening, or was this just something that happened by accident?

RA: I am Ra. This entity was, as your people put it, looking for a target of opportunity. The missed word was a chance occurrence and not a planned one.

We might suggest in the, shall we say, future, as you measure space/time, as you begin a working be aware that this instrument is likely being watched for any opportunity. Thus if the circle is walked with some imperfection, it is well to immediately repeat. The expelling of breath is also appropriate, always to the left.

QUESTIONER: Would you expand on what you just said on the expelling of the breath? I'm not quite sure of what you mean.

RA: I am Ra. The repetition of that performed well at this working is advisable if the circle is walked in less than the appropriate configuration.

QUESTIONER: But you mentioned the expelling of the breath to the left, I believe. Would you tell me what you meant by that?

RA: I am Ra. It is as you have just accomplished, the breath being sent above the instrument's head from its right side to its left.

QUESTIONER: Is there anything that we can do for the instrument after she comes out of the trance to help her recover from this attack?

RA: I am Ra. There is little to be done. You may watch to see if distortions persist, and see that the appropriate healers are brought into contact with this mind/body/spirit complex in the event that difficulty persists. It may not. This battle is even now being accomplished. Each may counsel the instrument to continue its work as outlined previously.

QUESTIONER: Who would the appropriate healers be, and how would we bring them in contact with the instrument?

RA: I am Ra. There are four. The difficulty being at all noticed as bodily distortion, the one known as [name of spiritual healer] and the one known as [name of spiritual healer] may work upon the instrument's bodily complex by means of the practices which are developing in each entity. Given persistence of distortion, the one known as [name of allopathic healer] shall be seen. Given the continued difficulty past the point of one of your cycles called the fortnight, the one known as [name of allopathic healer] shall be seen.

QUESTIONER: Does the instrument know who these people are, [name] and [name]? I don't know who they are?

RA: I am Ra. This is correct.

QUESTIONER: Is that the sum total of what we can do to aid the instrument?

RA: I am Ra. This is correct. We may note that the harmonies and loving social intercourse which prevails habitually in this group create a favorable environment for each of you to do your work.

QUESTIONER: What priority, shall I say, does the Orion group place on the reduction of effectiveness or elimination of effectiveness of this group with respect to activities on planet Earth at this time? Can you tell me that?

RA: I am Ra. This group, as all positive channels and supporting groups, is a greatly high priority with the Orion group. This instrument's bodily distortions are its most easily unbound or unloosed distortion dissolving the mind/body/spirit complex if the Orion group is successful; this particular group, having learned to be without serious chinks, may we say, in mind and spirit complex vibratory patterns. In other channels, other chinks may be more in evidence.

QUESTIONER: I'll make this statement and you correct it. The Orion group has an objective of the bringing of the service-to-self polarized entities to harvest, as great a harvest as possible. This harvest will build their potential or their ability to do work in consciousness as given by the distortion of the Law of One called the Law of Squares or Doubling. Is this correct?

RA: I am Ra. This is correct.

QUESTIONER: Are there other groups of those who are on the service-to-self path joined with those of the Orion constellation—for instance, those of Southern Cross—presently working for the same type of harvest with respect to Earth?

RA: I am Ra. These you mention of Southern Cross are members of the Orion group. It is not, shall we say, according to understood wording that a group from various galaxies should be named by one. However, those planetary social memory complexes of the so-called Orion constellation have the upper hand and thus rule the other members. You must recall that in negative thinking, there is always the pecking order, shall we say, and the power against power in separation.

QUESTIONER: By creating as large a harvest as possible of negatively oriented entities from Earth, then, the social memory complex of the Orion group gains in strength. Am I correct in assuming that this strength then is in the total strength of the complex, the pecking order remaining approximately the same, and those at the top gaining in strength with respect to the total strength of the social memory complex? Is this correct?

RA: I am Ra. This is correct. To the stronger go the greater shares of polarity.

QUESTIONER: Is this the fourth-density group that we are talking about now?

RA: I am Ra. There are fourth- and a few fifth-density members of the Orion group.

QUESTIONER: Then is the top of the pecking order fifth density?

RA: I am Ra. This is correct.

QUESTIONER: What is the objective; what does the leader, the one at the very top of the pecking order in fifth density of the Orion group, have as an objective? I would like to understand his philosophy with respect to his objectives and plans for what we might call the future or his future?

RA: I am Ra. This thinking will not be so strange to you. Therefore, we may speak through the densities, as your planet has some negatively oriented action in sway at this space/time nexus.

The early fifth-density negative entity, if oriented towards maintaining cohesion as a social memory complex, may in its free will determine that the path to wisdom lies in the manipulation in exquisite propriety of all other-selves. It then, by virtue of its abilities in wisdom, is able to be the leader of fourth-density beings which are upon the road to wisdom by exploring the dimensions of love of self and understanding of self. These fifth-density entities see the creation as that which shall be put in order.

Dealing with a plane such as this third density at this harvesting, it will see the mechanism of the call more clearly and have much less distortion towards plunder or manipulation by thoughts which are given to negatively oriented entities, although in allowing this to occur and sending less wise entities to do this work, any successes redound to the leaders.

The fifth density sees the difficulties posed by the light and in this way directs entities of this vibration to the seeking of targets of opportunity such as this one. If fourth-density temptations, shall we say, towards distortion of ego etc., are not successful, the fifth-density entity then thinks in terms of the removal of light.

QUESTIONER: When the Orion entity who waits us seeking the opportunity to attack is with us here, can you describe his method of coming here, what he looks like, and what his signs are? I know that this isn't too important, but it might give me a little insight into what we are talking about.

RA: I am Ra. Fifth-density entities are very light beings, although they do have the type of physical vehicle which you understand. Fifth-density entities are very fair to look upon in your standard of beauty.

The thought is what is sent for a fifth-density entity is likely to have mastered this technique or discipline. There is little or no means of perceiving such an entity, for unlike fourth-density negative entities, the fifth-density entity walks with light feet.

This instrument was aware of extreme coldness in the past diurnal cycle and spent much more time than your normal attitudes would imagine to be appropriate in what seemed to each of you an extremely warm climate. This was not perceived by the instrument, but the drop in subjective temperature is a sign of presence of a negative or non-positive or draining entity.

This instrument did mention a feeling of discomfort but was nourished by this group and was able to dismiss it. Had it not been for a random mishap, all would have been well, for you have learned to live in love and light and do not neglect to remember the One Infinite Creator.

QUESTIONER: Then it was a fifth-density entity that made this particular attack upon the instrument?

RA: I am Ra. This is correct.

QUESTIONER: Isn't this unusual that a fifth-density entity then would bother to do this rather than sending a fourth-density servant, shall I say?

RA: I am Ra. This is correct. Nearly all positive channels and groups may be lessened in their positivity or rendered quite useless by what we may call the temptations offered by the fourth-density negative thought-forms. They may suggest many distortions towards specific information, towards the aggrandizement of the self, towards the flowering of the organization in some political, social, or fiscal way.

These distortions remove the focus from the One Infinite Source of love and light of which we are all messengers, humble and knowing that we, of ourselves, are but the tiniest portion of the Creator, a small part of a magnificent entirety of infinite intelligence.

QUESTIONER: Is there something that the instrument could do or we could do for the instrument to eliminate the problems that she has, that she continually experiences of the cold feeling of these attacks?

RA: I am Ra. Yes.

QUESTIONER: Would you tell me what we could do?

RA: I am Ra. You could cease in your attempts to be channels for the love and the light of the One Infinite Creator.

QUESTIONER: Have I missed anything now that we can do at all to aid the instrument during, before, or after a session or at any time?

RA: I am Ra. The love and devotion of this group misses nothing. Be at peace. There is some toll for this work. This instrument embraces this or we could not speak. Rest then in that peace and love and do as you will, as you wish, as you feel. Let there be an end to worry when this is accomplished. The great healer of distortions is love.

QUESTIONER: I have a question that I didn't properly answer last night for [name]. It has to do with the vibrations of the densities. I understand that the first density is composed of core atomic vibrations that are in the red spectrum, second in the orange, etc. Am I to understand that the core vibrations of our planet are still in the red and that second-density beings are still in the orange at this space/time right now, and that each density as it exists on our planet right now has a different core vibration, or is this incorrect?

RA: I am Ra. This is precisely correct.

QUESTIONER: Then as the fourth-density vibrations come in, this means that the planet can support entities of fourth-density core vibration. Will the planet then still be first-density core vibration and will there be second-density entities on it with second-density vibrations, and will there be third-density entities on it with third-density vibrations?

RA: I am Ra. This will be the last full query of this working. There is energy, but the distortions of the instrument suggest to us it would be well to shorten this working with your permission.

QUESTIONER: Yes.

RA: You must see the Earth, as you call it, as being seven Earths. There is red, orange, yellow, and there will soon be a completed green-color vibratory locus for fourth-density entities which they will call Earth. During the fourth-density experience, due to the lack of development of fourth-density entities, the third-density planetary sphere is not useful for habitation, since the early fourth-density entity will not know precisely how to maintain the illusion that fourth density cannot be seen or determined from any instrumentation available to any third density.

Thus in fourth density the red, orange, and green energy nexi of your planet will be activated while the yellow is in potentiation along with the blue and the indigo.

May we ask at this time if there be any brief queries?

QUESTIONER: Is there anything that we can do to make the instrument more comfortable or to improve the contact?

RA: All is well. You have been most conscientious.

I am Ra. I leave you, my friends, in the glory of the love and the light of the One Infinite Creator. Go forth, then, rejoicing in the power and the peace of the One Infinite Creator. Adonai.

Session 63,
July 18, 1981

RA: I am Ra. I greet you in the love and in the light of the One Infinite Creator. We communicate now.

QUESTIONER: Could you give me an indication of the condition of the instrument?

RA: I am Ra. This instrument's vital energies are at the distortion which is normal for this mind/body/spirit complex. The body complex is distorted due to psychic attack in the area of the kidneys and urinary tract. There is also distortion continuing due to the distortion called arthritis.

You may expect this psychic attack to be constant, as this instrument has been under observation by negatively oriented force for some time.

QUESTIONER: Is the necessity of the instrument to go to the bathroom several times before a session due to the psychic attack?

RA: I am Ra. In general this is incorrect. The instrument is eliminating from the body complex the distortion leavings of the material which we use for contact. This occurs variably, sometimes beginning before contact, other workings this occurring after the contact.

In this particular working, this entity is experiencing the aforementioned difficulties causing the intensification of that particular distortion/condition.

QUESTIONER: I know that you have already answered this question, but I feel it my duty now to ask it each time in case there is some new development, and that is, is there anything that we can do that we aren't doing to lessen the effectiveness of the psychic attack upon the instrument?

RA: I am Ra. Continue in love and praise and thanksgiving to the Creator. Examine previous material. Love is the great protector.

QUESTIONER: Could you give me a definition of vital energy?

RA: I am Ra. Vital energy is the complex of energy levels of mind, body, and spirit. Unlike physical energy, it requires the integrated complexes vibrating in an useful manner.

The faculty of will can, to a variable extent, replace missing vital energy, and this has occurred in past workings, as you measure time, in this instrument. This is not recommended. At this time, however, the vital energies are well nourished in mind and spirit, although the physical energy level is, in and of itself, low at this time.

QUESTIONER: Would I be correct in guessing that the vital energy is a function of the awareness or bias of the entity with respect to his polarity or general unity with the Creator or creation?

RA: I am Ra. In a nonspecific sense we may affirm the correctness of your statement. The vital energy may be seen to be that deep love of life or life experiences such as the beauty of creation and the appreciation of other-selves and the distortions of your co-Creators' making which are of beauty.

Without this vital energy, the least distorted physical complex will fail and perish. With this love or vital energy or élan, the entity may continue though the physical complex is greatly distorted.

QUESTIONER: I would like to continue with the questions about the fact that in fourth density the red, orange, and green energies will be activated, yellow, blue, etc., being in potentiation. Right now, we have green energies activated. They have been activated for the last forty-five years. I am wondering about the transition through this period so that the green is totally activated and the yellow is in potentiation. What will we lose as the yellow goes from activation into potentiation, and what will we gain as green comes into total activation, and what is the process?

RA: I am Ra. It is misleading to speak of gains and losses when dealing with the subject of the cycle's ending and the green-ray cycle beginning upon your sphere. It is to be kept in the forefront of the faculties of intelligence that there is one creation in which there is no loss. There are progressive cycles for experiential use by entities. We may now address your query.

As the green-ray cycle or the density of love and understanding begins to take shape, the yellow-ray plane or Earth which you now enjoy in your dance will cease to be inhabited for some period of your space/time as the space/time necessary for fourth-density entities to learn their ability to shield their density from that of third is learned. After this period there will come a time when third density may again cycle on the yellow-ray sphere.

Meanwhile there is another sphere, congruent to a great extent with yellow ray, forming. This fourth-density sphere coexists with first, second, and third. It is of a denser nature due to the rotational core atomic aspects of its material. We have discussed this subject with you.

The fourth-density entities which incarnate at this space/time are fourth density in the view of experience but are incarnating in less dense vehicles due to desire to experience and aid in the birth of fourth density upon this plane.

You may note that fourth-density entities have a great abundance of compassion.

QUESTIONER: At present we have, in third-density incarnation on this plane, those third-density entities of the planet Earth who have been here for some number of incarnations who will graduate in the three-way split, either positive polarity remaining for fourth-density experience on this planet, the negative polarity harvestable going to another planet, and the rest unharvestable third density going to another third-density planet. In addition to these entities I am assuming that we have here some entities already harvestable from other third-density planets who have come here and have incarnated in third-density form to make the transition with this planet into fourth density, plus Wanderers.

Is this correct?

RA: I am Ra. This is correct except we may note a small point. The positively oriented harvested entities will remain in this planetary influence, but not upon this plane.

QUESTIONER: I think you said there were sixty million Wanderers, approximately, here now. Am I correct in that memory?

RA: I am Ra. This is approximately correct. There is some excess to that amount.

QUESTIONER: Does that number include the harvestable entities who are coming to this planet for the fourth-density experience?

RA: I am Ra. No.

QUESTIONER: Approximately how many are here now who have come here from other planets who are third-density harvestable for fourth-density experience?

RA: I am Ra. This is a recent, shall we say, phenomenon, and the number is not yet in excess of 35,000 entities.

QUESTIONER: Now these entities incarnate into a third-density vibratory body. I am trying to understand how this transition takes place from third to fourth density. I will take the example of one of these entities of which we are speaking who is now in a third-density body. He will grow older, and then will it be necessary that he die from the third-density physical body and reincarnate in a fourth-density body for that transition?

RA: I am Ra. These entities are those incarnating with what you may call a double body in activation. It will be noted that the entities birthing these fourth-density entities experience a great feeling of, shall we say, the connection and the use of spiritual energies during pregnancy. This is due to the necessity for manifesting the double body.
This transitional body is one which will be, shall we say, able to appreciate fourth-density vibratory complexes as the instreaming increases without the accompanying disruption of the third-density body. If a third-density entity were, shall we say, electrically aware of fourth density in full, the third-density electrical fields would fail due to incompatibility.
To answer your query about death, these entities will die according to third-density necessities.

QUESTIONER: You are saying, then, that for the transition from third to fourth density for one of the entities with doubly activated bodies, in order to make the transition the third-density body will go through the process of what we call death. Is this correct?

RA: I am Ra. The third and fourth, combination, density's body will die according to the necessity of third-density mind/body/spirit complex distortions.

We may respond to the heart of your question by noting that the purpose of such combined activation of mind/body/spirit complexes is that such entities, to some extent, conscientiously are aware of those fourth-density understandings which third density is unable to remember due to the forgetting. Thus fourth-density experience may be begun with the added attraction to an entity oriented toward service to others of dwelling in a troubled third-density environment and offering its love and compassion.

QUESTIONER: Would the purpose in transitioning to Earth prior to the complete changeover then be for the experience to be gained here before the harvesting process?

RA: I am Ra. This is correct. These entities are not Wanderers in the sense that this planetary sphere is their fourth-density home planet. However, the experience of this service is earned only by those harvested third-density entities which have demonstrated a great deal of orientation towards service to others. It is a privilege to be allowed this early an incarnation, as there is much experiential catalyst in service to other-selves at this harvesting.

QUESTIONER: There are many children now who have demonstrated the ability to bend metal mentally, which is a fourth-density phenomenon. Would most of these children, then, be the type of entity of which we speak?

RA: I am Ra. This is correct.

QUESTIONER: Is the reason that they can do this and the fifth-density Wanderers who are here cannot do it, the fact that they have the fourth-density body in activation?

RA: I am Ra. This is correct. Wanderers are third density activated in mind/body/spirit and are subject to the forgetting, which can only be penetrated with disciplined meditation and working.

QUESTIONER: I am assuming that the reason for this is, first, since the entities of harvestable third density who very recently have been coming here are coming here late enough so that they will not affect the polarization through their teachings. They are not infringing upon the first distortion because they are children now, and they won't be old enough to really affect any of the polarization until the transition is well advanced. However, the Wanderers who have come here are older and have a greater ability to affect the polarization. They must do their affecting as a function of their ability to penetrate the forgetting process in order to be within the first distortion. Is this correct?

RA: I am Ra. This is quite correct.

QUESTIONER: It would seem to me that some of the harvestable third-density entities are, however, relatively old, since I know of some individuals who can bend metal who are over fifty years old, and some others over thirty. Would there be other entities who could bend metal for other reasons than having dual-activated bodies?

RA: I am Ra. This is correct. Any entity who, by accident or by careful design, penetrates intelligent energy's gateway may use the shaping powers of this energy.

QUESTIONER: Now as this transition continues into fourth-density activation, in order to inhabit this fourth-density sphere it will be necessary for all third-density physical bodies to go through the process which we refer to as death. Is this correct?

RA: I am Ra. This is correct.

QUESTIONER: Are there any inhabitants at this time of this fourth-density sphere who have already gone through this process? Is it now being populated?

RA: I am Ra. This is correct only in the very, shall we say, recent past.

QUESTIONER: I would assume that this population is from other planets since the harvesting has not yet occurred on this planet. It is from planets where the harvesting has already occurred. Is this correct?

RA: I am Ra. This is correct.

QUESTIONER: Then are these entities visible to us? Could I see one of them? Would he walk upon our surface?

RA: I am Ra. We have discussed this. These entities are in dual bodies at this time.

QUESTIONER: Sorry that I am so stupid on this, but this particular concept is very difficult for me to understand. It is something that I am afraid requires some rather dumb questions on my part to fully understand, and I don't think I will ever fully understand it or even get a good grasp of it.

Then as the fourth-density sphere is activated, there is heat energy being generated. I assume that this heat energy is generated on the third-density sphere only. Is this correct?

RA: I am Ra. This is quite correct. The experiential distortions of each dimension are discrete.

QUESTIONER: Then at some time in the future, the fourth-density sphere will be fully activated. What is the difference between full activation and partial activation for this sphere?

RA: I am Ra. At this time the cosmic influxes are conducive to true color green core particles being formed and material of this nature thus being formed. However, there is a mixture of the yellow-ray and green-ray environments at this time, necessitating the birthing of transitional mind/body/spirit complex types of energy distortions. At full activation of the true color green density of love, the planetary sphere will be solid and inhabitable upon its own, and the birthing that takes place will have been transformed through the process of time, shall we say, to the appropriate type of vehicle to appreciate in full the fourth-density planetary environment. At this nexus the green-ray environment exists to a far greater extent in time/space than in space/time.

QUESTIONER: Could you describe the difference that you are speaking of with respect to time/space and space/time?

RA: I am Ra. For the sake of your understanding, we will use the working definition of inner planes. There is a great deal of subtlety invested in this sound vibration complex, but it, by itself, will perhaps fulfill your present need.

QUESTIONER: I will make this statement and have you correct me. What we have is, as our planet is spiraled by the spiraling action of the entire major galaxy and our planetary system spirals into the new position, the fourth-density vibrations becoming more and more pronounced. These atomic core vibrations begin to create, more and more completely, the fourth-density sphere and the fourth-density bodily complexes for inhabitation of that sphere. Is this correct?

RA: I am Ra. This is partially correct. To be corrected is the concept of the creation of green-ray-density bodily complexes. This creation will be gradual and will take place beginning with your third-density type of physical vehicle and, through the means of bisexual reproduction, become by evolutionary processes the fourth-density body complexes.

QUESTIONER: Then are these entities of whom we have spoken the third-density harvestable who have been transferred, the ones who then will, by bisexual reproduction, create the fourth-density complexes that are necessary?

RA: I am Ra. The influxes of true color green energy complexes will more and more create the conditions in which the atomic structure of cells of bodily complexes is that of the density of love. The mind/body/spirit complexes inhabiting these physical vehicles will be and, to some extent, are those of whom you spoke, and, as harvest is completed, the harvested entities of this planetary influence.

QUESTIONER: Is there a clock-like face, shall I say, associated with the entire major galaxy so that as it revolves it carries all of these stars and planetary systems through transitions from density to density? Is this how it works?

RA: I am Ra. You are perceptive. You may see a three-dimensional clockface or spiral of endlessness which is planned by the Logos for this purpose.

QUESTIONER: I understand that the Logos did not plan for the heating effect in our third-density transition into fourth. Is this correct?

RA: I am Ra. This is correct except for the condition of free will, which is, of course, planned by the Logos as It, Itself, is a creature of free will. In this climate an infinity of events or conditions may occur. They cannot be said to be planned by the Logos but can be said to have been freely allowed.

QUESTIONER: It would seem to me that the heating effect that takes place on the planet is analogous to a disease in the body and would have as a root cause the same or analogous mental configuration. Is this correct?

RA: I am Ra. This is correct except that the spiritual configuration as well as mental biases of your peoples has been responsible for these distortions of the body complex of your planetary sphere.

QUESTIONER: When the third density goes out of activation and into potentiation, that will leave us with a planet that is first, second, and fourth density. At that time there will be no activated third-density vibrations on this planet. Am I correct in assuming that all third-density vibrations on this planet now are those vibrations that compose the bodily complexes of entities such as we are; that that is the sum total of third-density vibrations on this planet at this time?

RA: I am Ra. This will be the last full query of this working. This instrument has energy left due to transfer, but there is discomfort. We do not wish to deplete this instrument. May we say that this instrument seems in better configuration despite attack than previous workings.

To answer your query, this is incorrect only in that in addition to the mind/body/spirit complexes of third density, there are the artifacts, thought-forms, and feelings which these co-Creators have produced. This is third density.

May we answer any brief queries as we leave this instrument?

QUESTIONER: Is there anything that we can do to make the instrument more comfortable or to improve the contact?

RA: I am Ra. You are conscientious. All is well. We leave you now, my friends, in the glory of the love and the light of the One Infinite Creator. Go forth, then, rejoicing in the power and the peace of the Infinite Creator. Adonai.

Session 64,
July 26, 1981

RA: I am Ra. I greet you in the love and in the light of the One Infinite Creator. We communicate now.

QUESTIONER: Could you first tell me the condition of the instrument?

RA: I am Ra. It is as previously stated, with the exception of a transitory distortion lessening the free flow of vital energy.

QUESTIONER: Can you tell me what the transitory distortion is?

RA: I am Ra. This is marginal information.

QUESTIONER: Then we won't question on it.
Could you explain the basic principles behind the ritual which we perform to initiate the contact and what I would call the basic white magical principles of protection?

RA: I am Ra. Due to your avenue of question, we perceive the appropriateness of inclusion of the cause of this instrument's transitory vital energy distortion. The cause is a bias towards the yearning for expression of devotion to the One Creator in group worship.
This entity was yearning for this protection both consciously in that it responds to the accoutrements of this expression, the ritual, the colors, and their meanings as given by the distortion system of what you call the church, the song of praise, and the combined prayers of thanksgiving and, most of all, that which may be seen to be most centrally magical, the intake of that food which is not of this dimension but has been transmuted into metaphysical nourishment in what this distortion of expression calls the holy communion.
The subconscious reason, it being the stronger for this yearning, was the awareness that such expression is, when appreciated by an entity as the transmutation into the presence of the One Creator, a great protection of the entity as it moves in the path of service to others.
The principle behind any ritual of the white magical nature is to so configure the stimuli which reach down into the trunk of mind that this arrangement causes the generation of disciplined and purified emotion or love which then may be both protection and the key to the gateway to intelligent infinity.

QUESTIONER: Can you tell me why the slight error made in the ritual starting this communication two sessions ago allowed the intrusion by an Orion-affiliated entity?

RA: I am Ra. This contact is narrow band and its preconditions precise. The other-self offering its service in the negative path also is possessed of the skill of the swordsman. You deal in this contact with, shall we say, forces of great intensity poured into a vessel as delicate as a snow-flake and as crystalline.

The smallest of lapses may disturb the regularity of this pattern of energies which forms the channel for these transmissions.

We may note for your information that our pause was due to the necessity of being quite sure that the mind/body/spirit complex of the instrument was safely in the proper light configuration or density before we dealt with the situation. Far better would it be to allow the shell to become unviable than to allow the mind/body/spirit complex to be, shall we say, misplaced.

QUESTIONER: Could you describe or tell me of rituals or techniques used by Ra in seeking in the direction of service?

RA: I am Ra. To speak of that which sixth-density social memory complexes labor within in order to advance is at best misprision of plain communication, for much is lost in transmission of concept from density to density, and the discussion of sixth density is inevitably distorted greatly.

However, we shall attempt to speak to your query, for it is a helpful one in that it allows us to express once again the total unity of creation. We seek the Creator upon a level of shared experience to which you are not privy, and rather than surrounding ourselves in light, we have become light. Our understanding is that there is no other material except light. Our rituals, as you may call them, are an infinitely subtle continuation of the balancing processes which you are now beginning to experience.

We seek now without polarity. Thus we do not invoke any power from without, for our search has become internalized as we become light/love and love/light. These are the balances we seek, the balances between compassion and wisdom which more and more allow our understanding of experience to be informed that we may come closer to the unity with the One Creator which we so joyfully seek.

Your rituals at your level of progress contain the concept of polarization, and this is most central at your particular space/time.

We may answer further if you have specific queries.

QUESTIONER: Would it be helpful if Ra were to describe the techniques that Ra used while Ra was third density to evolve in mind, body, and spirit?

RA: I am Ra. This query lies beyond the Law of Confusion.

QUESTIONER: What about fourth-density experience of Ra? Would that also lie beyond the Law of Confusion?

RA: I am Ra. This is correct. Let us express a thought. Ra is not elite. To speak of our specific experiences to a group which honors us is to guide to the point of a specific advising. Our work was that of your people, of experiencing the catalyst of joys and sorrows. Our circumstances were somewhat more harmonious. Let it be said that any entity or group may create the most splendid harmony in any outer atmosphere. Ra's experiences are no more than your own. Yours is the dance at this space/time in third-density harvest.

QUESTIONER: The question was brought up recently having to do with possible records left near, in, or under the Great Pyramid at Giza. I have no idea whether this would be of benefit. I will just ask if there is any benefit in investigating in this area?

RA: I am Ra. We apologize for seeming to be so shy of information. However, any words upon this particular subject create the possibility of infringement upon free will.

QUESTIONER: In a previous session you mentioned the gateway of magic for the adept occurring in eighteen-day cycles. Could you expand on that information, please?

RA: I am Ra. The mind/body/spirit complex is born under a series of influences, both lunar, planetary, cosmic, and in some cases, karmic. The moment of the birthing into this illusion begins the cycles we have mentioned.

The spiritual or adept's cycle is an eighteen-day cycle and operates with the qualities of the sine wave. Thus there are a few excellent days on the positive side of the curve, that being the first nine days of the cycle—precisely the fourth, the fifth, and the sixth—when workings are most appropriately undertaken, given that the entity is still without total conscious control of its mind/body/spirit distortion/ reality.

The most interesting portion of this information, like that of each cycle, is the noting of the critical point wherein passing from the ninth to the tenth and from the eighteenth to the first days the adept will experience some difficulty especially when there is a transition occurring in another cycle at the same time. At the nadir of each cycle the adept will be at its least powerful but will not be open to difficulties in nearly the degree that it experiences at critical times.

QUESTIONER: Then to find the cycles we would take the instant of birth and the emerging of the infant from the mother into this density and start the cycle at that instant and continue it through the life. Is this correct?

RA: I am Ra. This is mostly correct. It is not necessary to identify the instant of birthing. The diurnal cycle upon which this event occurs is satisfactory for all but the most fine workings.

QUESTIONER: Am I correct in assuming that whatever magic the adept would perform at this time would be more successful or, shall we say, more to his design than that performed at less opportune times in the cycle?

RA: I am Ra. This cycle is a helpful tool to the adept, but as we said, as the adept becomes more balanced, the workings designed will be dependent less and less upon these cycles of opportunity and more and more even in their efficacy.

QUESTIONER: I have no ability to judge at what point the level of abilities of the adept would be reached to be independent of this cyclical action. Can you give me an indication of what level of "adeptness" that would be necessary in order to be so independent?

RA: I am Ra. We are fettered from speaking specifically due to this group's work, for to speak would seem to be to judge. However, we may say that you may consider this cycle in the same light as the so-called astrological balances within your group; that is, they are interesting but not critical.

QUESTIONER: Thank you. I read that recent research has indicated that the normal sleep cycle for entities on this planet occurs one hour later each diurnal period, so that we have a twenty-five-hour cycle instead of a twenty-four-hour cycle. Is this correct, and if so, why is this?

RA: I am Ra. This is in some cases correct. The planetary influences from which those of Mars experience memory have some effect upon these third-density physical bodily complexes. This race has given its genetic material to many bodies upon your plane.

QUESTIONER: Thank you. Ra mentioned the ones [name] and [name] in a previous session. These are members of what we call our medical profession. What is the value of modern medical techniques in alleviating bodily distortions with respect to the purpose for these distortions and what we might call karma?

RA: I am Ra. This query is convoluted. However, we shall make some observations in lieu of attempting one coherent answer, for that which is allopathic among your healing practices is somewhat two-sided.

Firstly, you must see the possibility/probability that each and every allopathic healer is in fact a healer. Within your cultural nexus, this training is considered the appropriate means of perfecting the healing ability. In the most basic sense, any allopathic healer may be seen to, perhaps, be one whose desire is service to others in alleviation of bodily complex and mental/emotional complex distortions so that the entity to be healed may experience further catalyst over a longer period of what you call the life. This is a great service to others when appropriate due to the accumulation of distortions toward wisdom and love which can be created through the use of the space/time continuum of your illusion.

In observing the allopathic concept of the body complex as a machine, we may note the symptomology of a societal complex seemingly dedicated to the most intransigent desire for the distortions of distraction, anonymity, and sleep. This is the result rather than the cause of societal thinking upon your plane.

In turn this mechanical concept of the body complex has created the continuing proliferation of distortions towards what you would call ill health, due to the strong chemicals used to control and hide bodily distortions. There is a realization among many of your peoples that there are more efficacious systems of healing not excluding the allopathic but also including the many other avenues of healing.

QUESTIONER: Let us assume that a bodily distortion occurs within a particular entity who then has a choice of seeking allopathic aid or experiencing the catalyst of the distortion and not seeking correction of the distortion. Can you comment on the two possibilities for this entity and his analysis of each path?

RA: I am Ra. If the entity is polarized towards service to others, analysis properly proceeds along the lines of consideration of which path offers the most opportunity for service to others.

For the negatively polarized entity, the antithesis is the case.

For the unpolarized entity, the considerations are random and most likely in the direction of the distortion towards comfort.

QUESTIONER: I understand [name] brought a four-toed Bigfoot cast by here the other day. Could you tell me which form of Bigfoot that cast was?

RA: I am Ra. We can.

QUESTIONER: I know that it is totally unimportant, but as a service to [name], I thought that I should ask that.

RA: I am Ra. This entity was one of a small group of thought-forms.

QUESTIONER: He also asked—I know this is also unimportant— why there were no Bigfoot remains found after the entities have died on our surface. Could you also answer this? I know this is of no importance, but as a service to him I ask it.

RA: I am Ra. You may suggest that exploration of the caves which underlie some of the western coastal mountain regions of your continent will one day offer such remains. They will not be generally understood if this culture survives in its present form long enough in your time measurement for this probability/possibility vortex to occur.
　There is enough energy for one more full query at this time.

QUESTIONER: In the healing exercises, when you say examine the sensations of the body, do you mean those sensations available to the body via the five senses or in relation to the natural functions of the body such as touching, loving, sexual sharing, and company, or are you speaking of something else altogether?

RA: I am Ra. The questioner may perceive its body complex at this moment. It is experiencing sensations. Most of these sensations or, in this case, nearly all of them are transient and without interest. However, the body is the creature of the mind. Certain sensations carry importance due to the charge or power which is felt by the mind upon the experience of this sensation.
　For instance, at this space/time nexus, one sensation is carrying a powerful charge and may be examined. This is the sensation of what you call the distortion towards discomfort due to the cramped position of the body complex during this working. In balancing you would then explore this sensation. Why is this sensation powerful? Because it was chosen in order that the entity might be of service to others in energizing this contact.

Each sensation that leaves the aftertaste of meaning upon the mind, that leaves the taste within the memory, shall be examined. These are the sensations of which we speak.

May we answer any brief queries before we leave this instrument?

QUESTIONER: Is there anything that we could do to make the instrument more comfortable or to improve the contact?

RA: I am Ra. Continue to consider the alignments. You are conscientious and aware of the means of caring for the instrument in its present distortions having to do with the wrists and hands. As always, love is the greatest protection.

I am Ra. I leave you, my friends, in the glorious love and joyful light of the Infinite Creator. Go forth, then, rejoicing in the power and in the peace of the One Infinite Creator. Adonai.

Session 65,
August 8, 1981

RA: I am Ra. I greet you in the love and in the light of the One Infinite Creator. We communicate now.

QUESTIONER: Could you first please give us an indication of the instrument's condition and the level of vital and physical energies?

RA: I am Ra. This instrument's vital energies are as previously stated. The physical energies are greatly distorted towards weakness at this space/time due to the distortion complexes symptomatic of that which you call the arthritic condition. The level of psychic attack is constant but is being dealt with by this instrument in such a way as to eliminate serious difficulties due to its fidelity and that of the support group.

QUESTIONER: I may be recovering a little ground already covered today, but I am trying to get a more clear picture of some things that I don't understand, and possibly develop a plan of my own for activity in the future.

I have the impression that in the near future the seeking will increase by many who now are incarnate in the physical on this planet. Their seeking will increase because they will become more aware of the creation as it is and as it is opposed, I might say, to the creation of man. Their orientation and their thinking will be, by catalyst of a unique nature, reoriented to thinking of more basic concepts, shall I say. Is this correct?

RA: I am Ra. The generalities of expression can never be completely correct. However, we may note that when faced with a hole in the curtain, an entity's eyes may well peer for the first time through the window beyond. This tendency is probable given the possibility/probability vortices active within your space/time and time/space continua at this nexus.

QUESTIONER: I have assumed that the reason that so many Wanderers and those harvested third-density entities who have been transferred here find it a privilege and an exceptionally beneficial time to be incarnate upon this planet is that the effect that I just spoke of gives them the opportunity to be more fully of service because of the increased seeking. Is this, in general, correct?

RA: I am Ra. This is the intention which Wanderers had prior to incarnation. There are many Wanderers whose dysfunction with regard to the planetary ways of your peoples have caused, to some extent, a condition of being caught up in a configuration of mind complex activity which, to the corresponding extent, may prohibit the intended service.

QUESTIONER: I noticed that you are speaking more slowly than usual. Is there a reason for this?

RA: I am Ra. This instrument is somewhat weak and, although strong in vital energy and well able to function at this time, is somewhat more fragile than the usual condition we find. We may note a continuing bearing of the physical distortion called pain, which has a weakening effect upon physical energy. In order to use the considerable store of available energy without harming the instrument, we are attempting to channel even more narrow band than is our wont.

QUESTIONER: Have I properly analyzed the condition that creates the possibility of greater service as follows: Seniority by vibration of incarnation has greatly polarized those upon the surface of the planet now, and the influx of Wanderers has greatly increased the mental configuration toward things of a more spiritual nature. This would be, I assume, one of the factors creating a better atmosphere for service. Is this correct?

RA: I am Ra. This is correct.

QUESTIONER: Would the coming changes as we progress into fourth density, such as changes in the physical third-density planet due to the heating effect and changes such as the ability of people to perform what we term paranormal activities, act as catalyst to create a greater seeking?

RA: I am Ra. This is partially correct. The paranormal events occurring are not designed to increase seeking but are manifestations of those whose vibratory configuration enables these entities to contact the gateway to intelligent infinity. These entities capable of paranormal service may determine to be of such service on a conscious level. This, however, is a function of the entity and its free will and not the paranormal ability.

The correct portion of your statements is the greater opportunity for service due to the many changes which will offer many challenges, difficulties, and seeming distresses within your illusion to many who then will seek to understand, if we may use this misnomer, the reason for the malfunctioning of the physical rhythms of their planet.

Moreover, there exists probability/possibility vortices which spiral towards your bellicose actions. Many of these vortices are not of the nuclear war but of the less annihilatory but more lengthy so-called "conventional" war. This situation, if formed in your illusion, would offer many opportunities for seeking and for service.

QUESTIONER: How would conventional warfare offer the opportunities for seeking and service?

RA: I am Ra. The possibility/probabilities exist for situations in which great portions of your continent and the globe in general might be involved in the type of warfare which you might liken to guerrilla warfare. The ideal of freedom from the so-called invading force of either the controlled fascism or the equally controlled social common ownership of all things would stimulate great quantities of contemplation upon the great polarization implicit in the contrast between freedom and control. In this scenario which is being considered at this time/space nexus, the idea of obliterating valuable sites and personnel would not be considered a useful one. Other weapons would be used which do not destroy as your nuclear arms would. In this ongoing struggle, the light of freedom would burn within the mind/body/spirit complexes capable of such polarization. Lacking the opportunity for overt expression of the love of freedom, the seeking for inner knowledge would take root aided by those of the Brothers and Sisters of Sorrow which remember their calling upon this sphere.

QUESTIONER: We would seem to have dual catalysts operating, and the question is which one is going to act first. The prophecies, I will call them, made by Edgar Cayce indicated many Earth changes, and I am wondering about the mechanics describing the future. Ra, it has been stated, is not a part of time, and yet we concern ourselves with possibility/probability vortices. It is very difficult for me to understand how the mechanism of prophecy operates. What is the value of such a prophecy such as Cayce made with respect to Earth changes and all of these scenarios?

RA: I am Ra. Consider the shopper entering the store to purchase food with which to furnish the table for the time period you call a week. Some stores have some items, others a variant set of offerings. We speak of these possibility/probability vortices when asked with the understanding that such are as a can, jar, or portion of goods in your store.

It is unknown to us as we scan your time/space whether your peoples will shop hither or yon. We can only name some of the items available for the choosing. The, shall we say, record which the one you call Edgar read from is useful in that same manner. There is less knowledge in this material of other possibility/probability vortices and more attention paid to the strongest vortex. We see the same vortex but also see many others. Edgar's material could be likened unto one hundred boxes of your cold cereal, another vortex likened unto three, or six, or fifty of another product which is eaten by your peoples for breakfast. That you will breakfast is close to certain. The menu is your own choosing.

The value of prophecy must be realized to be only that of expressing possibilities. Moreover, it must be, in our humble opinion, carefully taken into consideration that any time/space viewing, whether by one of your time/space or by one such as we who view the time/space from a dimension, shall we say, exterior to it will have a quite difficult time expressing time measurement values. Thus prophecy given in specific terms is more interesting for the content or type of possibility predicted than for the space/time nexus of its supposed occurrence.

QUESTIONER: So we have the distinct possibility of two different types of catalyst creating an atmosphere of seeking that is greater than that which we experience at present. There will be much confusion, especially in the scenario of Earth changes, simply because there have been many predictions of these changes by many groups, giving many and sundry reasons for the changes. Can you comment on the effectiveness of this type of catalyst and the rather wide pre-knowledge of the coming changes but also the wide variation in explanation for these changes?

RA: I am Ra. Given the amount of strength of the possibility/probability vortex which posits the expression by the planet itself of the difficult birthing of the planetary self into fourth density, it would be greatly surprising were not many which have some access to space/time able to perceive this vortex. The amount of this cold cereal in the grocery, to use our previous analogy, is disproportionately large. Each which prophesies does so from a unique level, position, or vibratory configuration. Thus biases and distortions will accompany much prophecy.

QUESTIONER: This entire scenario for the next twenty years seems to be aimed at producing an increase in seeking and an increase in the awareness of the natural creation, but also a terrific amount of confusion. Was it the pre-incarnative objective of many of the Wanderers to attempt to reduce this confusion?

RA: I am Ra. It was the aim of Wanderers to serve the entities of this planet in whatever way was requested, and it was also the aim of Wanderers that their vibratory patterns might lighten the planetary vibration as a whole, thus ameliorating the effects of planetary disharmony and palliating any results of this disharmony.

Specific intentions such as aiding in a situation not yet manifest are not the aim of Wanderers. Light and love go where they are sought and needed, and their direction is not planned aforetimes.

QUESTIONER: Then each of the Wanderers here acts as a function of the biases he has developed in any way he sees fit to communicate or simply be in his polarity to aid the total consciousness of the planet. Is there any physical way in which he aids, perhaps by his vibrations, somehow just adding to the planet just as electrical polarity or charging a battery? Does that also aid the planet, just the physical presence of the Wanderers?

RA: I am Ra. This is correct, and the mechanism is precisely as you state. We intended this meaning in the second portion of our previous answer.

You may, at this time, note that as with any entities, each

Wanderer has its unique abilities, biases, and specialties, so that from each portion of each density represented among the Wanderers come an array of pre-incarnative talents which then may be expressed upon this plane which you now experience, so that each Wanderer, in offering itself before incarnation, has some special service to offer in addition to the doubling effect of planetary love and light and the basic function of serving as beacon or shepherd.

Thus there are those of fifth density whose abilities to express wisdom are great. There are fourth- and sixth-density Wanderers whose ability to serve as, shall we say, passive radiators or broadcasters of love and love/light are immense. There are many others whose talents brought into this density are quite varied.

Thus, Wanderers have three basic functions once the forgetting is penetrated, the first two being basic, the tertiary one being unique to that particular mind/body/spirit complex.

We may note at this point while you ponder the possibility/probability vortices that although you have many, many items which cause distress and thus offer seeking and service opportunities, there is always one container in that store of peace, love, light, and joy. This vortex may be very small, but to turn one's back upon it is to forget the infinite possibilities of the present moment. Could your planet polarize towards harmony in one fine, strong moment of inspiration? Yes, my friends. It is not probable, but it is ever possible.

QUESTIONER: How common in the universe is a mixed harvest from a planet of both positively and negatively oriented mind/body/spirit complexes?

RA: I am Ra. Among planetary harvests which yield a harvest of mind/body/spirit complexes, approximately 10 percent are negative, approximately 60 percent are positive, and approximately 30 percent are mixed, with nearly all harvest being positive. In the event of mixed harvest, it is almost unknown for the majority of the harvest to be negative. When a planet moves strongly towards the negative, there is almost no opportunity for harvestable positive polarization.

QUESTIONER: Can you tell me why there is almost no opportunity in that case?

RA: The ability to polarize positively requires a certain degree of self-determination.

QUESTIONER: Then as these final days of the cycle transpire, if the harvest were to occur now, today, it would have a certain number harvested positively and negatively and a certain number of repeaters. I am going to assume that because of the catalyst that will be experienced between now and the actual harvesting time, these numbers of harvestable entities will increase.

Generally speaking, not particularly with respect to this planet but with respect to general experience in harvesting, how big an increase in harvestable entities can you logically assume will occur because of the catalyst that occurs in the final period such as this one, or am I making a mistake in assuming that other planets have added catalyst at the end of a harvesting period when they have a mixed harvest?

RA: I am Ra. In the event of mixed harvest, there is nearly always disharmony and, therefore, added catalyst in the form of your so-called "Earth changes." In this assumption you are correct.

It is the Confederation's desire to serve those who may indeed seek more intensely because of this added catalyst. We do not choose to attempt to project the success of added numbers to the harvest, for this would not be appropriate. We are servants. If we are called, we shall serve with all our strength. To count the numbers is without virtue.

QUESTIONER: Now the added catalyst at the end of the cycle is a function specifically of the orientation of the consciousness that inhabits the planet. The consciousness has provided the catalyst for itself in orienting its thinking in the way it has oriented it, thus acting upon itself the same as catalyst of bodily pain and disease act upon the single mind/body/spirit complex. I made this analogy once before but reiterate it at this time to clarify my own thinking in seeing the planetary entity as somewhat of a single entity made up of billions of mind/body/spirit complexes. Is my viewpoint correct?

RA: I am Ra. You are quite correct.

QUESTIONER: Then we deal with an entity that has not yet formed a social memory but is yet an entity just as one of us can be called a single entity. Can we continue this observation of the conglomerate entity through the galactic entity, or, shall I say, planetary system type of entity? Let me try to phrase it this way. Could I look at a single sun in its planetary system as an entity and then look at a major galaxy with its billions of stars as an entity? Can I continue this extrapolation in this way?

RA: I am Ra. You can, but not within the framework of third-density space/time.

Let us attempt to speak upon this interesting subject. In your space/time, you and your peoples are the parents of that which is in the womb. The Earth, as you call it, is ready to be born, and the delivery is not going smoothly. When this entity has become born, it will be instinct with the social memory complex of its parents which have become fourth-density positive. In this density there is a broader view.

You may begin to see your relationship to the Logos or sun with which you are most intimately associated. This is not the relationship of parent to child but of Creator, that is Logos, to Creator that is the mind/body/spirit complex, as Logos. When this realization occurs, you may then widen the field of "eyeshot," if you will, infinitely recognizing parts of the Logos throughout the one infinite creation and feeling, with the roots of mind informing the intuition, the parents aiding their planets in evolution in reaches vast and unknown in the creation, for this process occurs many, many times in the evolution of the creation as an whole.

QUESTIONER: The Wanderer goes through a forgetting process. You mentioned that those who have both third- and fourth-density bodies activated now do not have the forgetting that the Wanderer has. I was just wondering if, say, a sixth-density Wanderer were here with a third-density body activated, would he have gone through a forgetting that was in sections, shall I say, a forgetting of fourth, fifth, and sixth densities, and if he were to have his fourth-density body activated, then he would have a partial additional memory and then another partial memory if his fifth-density body were activated and full memory if he had his sixth-density body activated? Does this make any sense?

RA: I am Ra. No.

QUESTIONER: Thank you. The forgetting process was puzzling me because you said that the fourth-density activated people who were here who had been harvested did not have the same forgetting problem. Could you tell me why the Wanderer loses his memory?

RA: I am Ra. The reason is twofold. First, the genetic properties of the connection between the mind/body/spirit complex and the cellular structure of the body is different for third density than for third/fourth density.

Secondly, the free will of third-density entities needs be

preserved. Thus, Wanderers volunteer for third-density genetic or DNA connections to the mind/body/spirit complex. The forgetting process can be penetrated to the extent of the Wanderer remembering what it is and why it is upon the planetary sphere. However, it would be an infringement if Wanderers penetrated the forgetting so far as to activate the more dense bodies and thus be able to live, shall we say, in a godlike manner. This would not be proper for those who have chosen to serve.

The new fourth-density entities which are becoming able to demonstrate various newer abilities are doing so as a result of the present experience, not as a result of memory. There are always a few exceptions, and we ask your forgiveness for constant barrages of over-generalization.

QUESTIONER: I don't know if this question is related to what I am trying to get at or not. I'll ask it and see what results. You mentioned in speaking of the pyramids the resonating chamber was used so that the adept could meet the self. Would you explain what you meant by that?

RA: I am Ra. One meets the self in the center or deeps of the being. The so-called resonating chamber may be likened unto the symbology of the burial and resurrection of the body, wherein the entity dies to self and, through this confrontation of apparent loss and realization of essential gain, is transmuted into a new and risen being.

QUESTIONER: Could I make the analogy of in this apparent death of losing the desires that are the illusory, common desires of third density and gaining desires of total service to others?

RA: I am Ra. You are perceptive. This was the purpose and intent of this chamber, as well as forming a necessary portion of the King's Chamber position's effectiveness.

QUESTIONER: Can you tell me what this chamber did to the entity to create this awareness in him?

RA: I am Ra. This chamber worked upon the mind and the body. The mind was affected by sensory deprivation and the archetypical reactions to being buried alive with no possibility of extricating the self. The body was affected both by the mind configuration and by the electrical and piezoelectrical properties of the materials which were used in the construction of the resonating chamber.

This will be the last full query of this working. May we ask if there are any brief queries at this time?

QUESTIONER: Is there anything that we can do to make the instrument more comfortable or to improve the contact?

RA: I am Ra. We feel that the instrument is well supported and that all is well. We caution each regarding this instrument's distortions towards pain, for it dislikes sharing these expressions, but as support group this instrument subconsciously accepts each entity's aid. All is in alignment. You are conscientious. We thank you for this. I am Ra. I leave you, my friends, rejoicing in the love and the light of the One Infinite Creator. Go forth, therefore, glorying in the power and in the peace of the One Infinite Creator. Adonai.

Session 66,
August 12, 1981

RA: I am Ra. I greet you in the love and in the light of the One Infinite Creator. We communicate now.

QUESTIONER: I would like to investigate the mechanism of healing using the crystallized healer. I am going to make a statement, and I would appreciate it if you would correct my thinking.

It seems to me that once the healer has become properly balanced and unblocked with respect to energy centers, it is possible for him to act in some way as a collector and focuser of light in a way analogous to the way a pyramid works, collecting light through the left hand and emitting it through the right; this then, somehow, penetrating the first and seventh chakras' vibratory envelop of the body and allowing for the realignment of energy centers of the entity to be healed. I'm quite sure that I'm not completely correct on this, and possibly considerably off. Could you rearrange my thinking so that it makes sense?

RA: I am Ra. You are correct in your assumption that the crystallized healer is analogous to the pyramidal action of the King's Chamber position. There are a few adjustments we might suggest.

Firstly, the energy which is used is brought into the field complex of the healer by the outstretched hand used in a polarized sense. However, this energy circulates through the various points of energy to the base of the spine and, to a certain extent, the feet, thus coming through the main energy centers of the healer, spiraling through the feet, turning at the red energy center towards a spiral at the yellow energy center, and passing through the green energy center in a microcosm of the King's Chamber energy configuration of prana; this then continuing for the third spiral through the blue energy center and being sent therefrom through the gateway back to intelligent infinity.

It is from the green center that the healing prana moves into the polarized healing right hand and therefrom to the one to be healed.

We may note that there are some who use the yellow-ray configuration to transfer energy, and this may be done, but the effects are questionable and, with regard to the relationship between the healer, the healing energy, and the seeker, questionable due to the propensity for the seeker to continue requiring such energy transfers without any true healing taking place in the absence of the healer due to the lack of penetration of the armoring shell of which you spoke.

QUESTIONER: A Wanderer who has an origin from fifth or sixth density can attempt such a healing and have little or no results. Can you tell me what the Wanderer has lost and why it is necessary for him to regain certain balances and abilities for him to perfect his healing ability?

RA: I am Ra. You may see the Wanderer as the infant attempting to verbalize the sound complexes of your peoples. The memory of the ability to communicate is within the infant's undeveloped mind complex, but the ability to practice or manifest this, called speech, is not immediately forthcoming due to the limitations of the mind/body/spirit complex it has chosen to be a part of in this experience.

So it is with the Wanderer, which, remembering the ease with which adjustments can be made in the home density, yet still having entered third density, cannot manifest that memory due to the limitation of the chosen experience. The chances of a Wanderer being able to heal in third density are only more than those native to this density because the desire to serve may be stronger and this method of service chosen.

QUESTIONER: What about the ones with the dual type of activated third- and fourth-density bodies, harvested from other third-density planets? Are they able to heal using the techniques that we have discussed?

RA: I am Ra. In many cases this is so, but as beginners of fourth density, the desire may not be present.

QUESTIONER: I'm assuming, then, that we have a Wanderer with the desire attempting to learn the techniques of healing while, shall I say, trapped in third density. He then, it seems to me, is primarily concerned with the balancing and unblocking of the energy centers. Am I correct in this assumption?

RA: I am Ra. This is correct. Only insofar as the healer has become balanced may it be a channel for the balancing of an other-self. The healing is first practiced upon the self, if we may say this, in another way.

QUESTIONER: Now as the healer approaches an other-self to do the healing, we have a situation where the other-self has, through programming of catalyst, possibly created a condition which is viewed as a condition needing healing. What is the situation and what are the ramifications of the healer acting upon the condition of programmed catalyst to bring about healing? Am I correct in assuming that in doing this healing, the programmed catalyst is useful to the one to be healed in that the one to be healed then becomes aware of what it wished to become aware of in programming the catalyst? Is this correct?

RA: I am Ra. Your thinking cannot be said to be completely incorrect but shows a rigidity which is not apparent in the flow of the experiential use of catalyst.

The role of the healer is to offer an opportunity for realignment or aid in realignment of either energy centers or some connection between the energies of mind and body, spirit and mind, or spirit and body. This latter is very rare.

The seeker will then have the reciprocal opportunity to accept a novel view of the self, a variant arrangement of patterns of energy influx. If the entity, at any level, desires to remain in the configuration of distortion which seems to need healing, it will do so. If, upon the other hand, the seeker chooses the novel configuration, it is done through free will.

This is one great difficulty with other forms of energy transfer in that they do not carry through the process of free will, as this process is not native to yellow ray.

QUESTIONER: What is the difference, philosophically, between a mind/body/spirit complex healing itself through mental, shall I say, configuration and it being healed by a healer?

RA: I am Ra. You have a misconception. The healer does not heal. The crystallized healer is a channel for intelligent energy which offers an opportunity to an entity that it might heal itself.

In no case is there another description of healing. Therefore, there is no difference as long as the healer never approaches one whose request for aid has not come to it previously. This is also true of the more conventional healers of your culture, and if these healers could but fully realize that they are responsible only for offering the opportunity of healing, and not for the healing, many of these entities would feel an enormous load of misconceived responsibility fall from them.

QUESTIONER: Then in seeking healing, a mind/body/spirit complex would then be seeking in some cases a source of gathered and focused light energy. This source could be another mind/body/spirit complex sufficiently crystallized for this purpose or the pyramid shape, or possibly something else. Is this correct?

RA: I am Ra. These are some of the ways an entity may seek healing. Yes.

QUESTIONER: Could you tell me the other ways an entity could seek healing?

RA: I am Ra. Perhaps the greatest healer is within the self and may be tapped with continued meditation as we have suggested. The many forms of healing available to your peoples . . . each have virtue and may be deemed appropriate by any seeker who wishes to alter the physical complex distortions or some connection between the various portions of the mind/body/spirit complex thereby.

QUESTIONER: I have observed many activities known as psychic surgery in the area of the Philippine Islands. It was my assumption that these healers are providing what I would call a training aid or a way of creating a reconfiguration of the mind of the patient to be healed as the relatively naive patient observes the action of the healer in seeing the materialized blood etc., and reconfigures the roots of mind to believe, you might say, the healing is done, and, therefore, heals himself. Is this analysis that I have made correct?

RA: I am Ra. This is correct. We may speak slightly further on the type of opportunity.

There are times when the malcondition to be altered is without emotional, mental, or spiritual interest to the entity and is merely that which has, perhaps by chance genetic arrangement, occurred. In these cases, that which is apparently dematerialized will remain dematerialized and may be observed as so by any observer. The malcondition which has an emotional, mental, or spiritual charge is likely not to remain dematerialized in the sense of the showing of the objective referent to an observer. However, if the opportunity has been taken by the seeker, the apparent malcondition of the physical complex will be at variance with the actual health, as you call this distortion, of the seeker and the lack of experiencing the distortions which the objective referent would suggest still held sway.

For instance, in this instrument the removal of three small cysts was the removal of material having no interest to the entity. Thus these growths remained dematerialized after the so-called psychic surgery experience. In other psychic surgery, the kidneys of this instrument were carefully offered a new configuration of beingness which the entity embraced. However, this particular portion of the mind/body/spirit complex carried a great deal of emotional, mental, and spiritual charge due to this distorted functioning being the cause of great illness in a certain configuration of events which culminated in this entity's conscious decision to be of service. Therefore, any objective scanning of this entity's renal complex would indicate the rather extreme dysfunctional aspect which it showed previous to the psychic surgery experience, as you call it.

The key is not in the continuation of the dematerialization of distortion to the eye of the beholder but rather lies in the choosing of the newly materialized configuration which exists in time/space.

QUESTIONER: Would you explain that last comment about the configuration in time/space?

RA: I am Ra. Healing is done in the time/space portion of the mind/body/spirit complex, is adopted by the form-making or etheric body, and is then given to the space/time physical illusion for use in the activated yellow mind/body/spirit complex. It is the adoption of the configuration which you call health by the etheric body in time/space which is the key to what you call health, not any event which occurs in space/time. In the process you may see the transdimensional aspect of what you call will, for it is the will, the seeking, the desire of the entity which causes the indigo body to use the novel configuration and to reform the body which exists in space/time. This is done in an instant and may be said to operate without regard to time. We may note that in the healing of very young children, there is often an apparent healing by the healer in which the young entity has no part. This is never so, for the mind/body/spirit complex in time/space is always capable of willing the distortions it chooses for experience, no matter what the apparent age, as you call it, of the entity.

QUESTIONER: Is this desire and will that operates through to the time/space section a function only of the entity who is healed, or is it also the function of the healer, the crystallized healer?

RA: I am Ra. May we take this opportunity to say that this is the activity of the Creator. To specifically answer your query, the crystallized healer has no will. It offers an opportunity without attachment to the outcome, for it is aware that all is one and that the Creator is knowing Itself.

QUESTIONER: Then the desire must be strong in the mind/body/spirit complex who seeks healing to be healed in order for the healing to occur? Is this correct?

RA: I am Ra. This is correct on one level or another. An entity may not consciously seek healing and yet subconsciously be aware of the need to experience the new set of distortions which result from healing. Similarly, an entity may consciously desire healing greatly but within the being, at some level, find some cause whereby certain configurations which seem quite distorted are, in fact, at that level, considered appropriate.

QUESTIONER: I assume that the reason for assuming the distortions appropriate would be that these distortions would aid the entity in its reaching its ultimate objective, which is a movement along the path of evolution in the desired polarity. Is this correct?

RA: I am Ra. This is correct.

QUESTIONER: Then an entity who becomes aware of his polarization with respect to service to others might find a paradoxical situation in the case where it was unable to fully serve because of distortions chosen to reach the understanding it has reached. At this point it would seem that the entity who was aware of the mechanism might, through meditation, understand the necessary mental configuration for alleviating the physical distortion so that it could be of greater service to others. At this particular nexus, am I correct in this thinking?

RA: I am Ra. You are correct, although we might note that there are often complex reasons for the programming of a distorted physical complex pattern. In any case, meditation is always an aid to knowing the self.

QUESTIONER: Is a vertical positioning of the spine useful or helpful in the meditative procedure?

RA: I am Ra. It is somewhat helpful.

QUESTIONER: Would you please list the polarities within the body which are related to the balancing of the energy centers of the various bodies of the unmanifested entity?

RA: I am Ra. In this question there lies a great deal of thought, which we appreciate. It is possible that the question itself may serve to aid meditations upon this particular subject. Each unmanifested self is unique. The basic polarities have to do with the balanced vibratory rates and relationships between the first three energy centers and, to a lesser extent, each of the other energy centers.

May we answer more specifically?

QUESTIONER: Possibly in the next session we will expand on that.

I would like to ask the second question. What are the structure and contents of the archetypical mind, and how does the archetypical mind function in informing the intuition and conscious mind of an individual mind/body/spirit complex?

RA: I am Ra. You must realize that we offered these concepts to you so that you might grow in your own knowledge of the self through the consideration of them. We would prefer, especially for this latter query, to listen to the observations upon this subject which the student of these exercises may make, and then suggest further avenues of the refinement of these inquiries. We feel we might be of more aid in this way.

QUESTIONER: You mentioned that an energizing spiral is emitted from the top of any pyramid and that you could benefit by placing this under the head for a period of thirty minutes or less. Can you tell me how this third spiral is helpful and what help it gives the entity who is receiving it?

RA: I am Ra. There are substances which you may ingest which cause the physical vehicle to experience distortions towards an increase of energy. These substances are crude, working rather roughly upon the body complex increasing the flow of adrenalin.

The vibration offered by the energizing spiral of the pyramid is such that each cell, both in space/time and in time/space, is charged as if hooked to your electricity. The keenness of mind, the physical and sexual energy of body, and the attunement of will of spirit are all touched by this energizing influence. It may be used in any of these ways. It is possible to overcharge a battery, and this is the cause of our cautioning any who use such pyramidal energies to remove the pyramid after a charge has been received.

QUESTIONER: Is there a best material or an optimal size for this small pyramid to go beneath the head?

RA: I am Ra. Given that the proportions are such as to develop the spirals in the Giza pyramid, the most appropriate size for use beneath the head is an overall height small enough to make placing it under the cushion of the head a comfortable thing.

QUESTIONER: There's no best material?

RA: I am Ra. There are better materials which are, in your system of barter, quite dear. They are not that much better than substances which we have mentioned before. The only incorrect substances would be the baser metals.

QUESTIONER: You mentioned the problems with the action in the King's Chamber of the Giza-type pyramid. I am assuming if we used the same geometrical configuration that is used in the pyramid at Giza, this would be perfectly all right for the pyramid placed beneath the head, since we wouldn't be using the King's Chamber radiations but only the third spiral from the top, and I'm also asking if it would be better to use a 60° apex angle than the larger apex angle? Would it provide a better energy source?

RA: I am Ra. For energy through the apex angle the Giza pyramid offers an excellent model. Simply be sure the pyramid is so small that there is no entity small enough to crawl inside it.

QUESTIONER: I assume that this energy, then, this spiraling light energy, is somehow absorbed by the energy field of the body. Is this somehow connected to the indigo energy center? Am I correct in this guess?

RA: I am Ra. This is incorrect. The properties of this energy are such as to move within the field of the physical complex and irradiate each cell of the space/time body and, as this is done, irradiate also the time/space equivalent which is closely aligned with the space/time yellow-ray body. This is not a function of the etheric body or of free will. This is a radiation much like your sun's rays. Thus it should be used with care.

QUESTIONER: How many applications of thirty minutes or less during a diurnal time period would be appropriate?

RA: I am Ra. In most cases, no more than one. In a few cases, especially where the energy will be used for spiritual work, experimentation with two shorter periods might be possible, but any feeling of sudden weariness would be a sure sign that the entity had been over-radiated.

QUESTIONER: Can this energy help in any way as far as healing of physical distortions?

RA: I am Ra. There is no application for direct healing using this energy, although, if used in conjunction with meditation, it may offer to a certain percentage of entities some aid in meditation. In most cases it is most helpful in alleviating weariness and in the stimulation of physical or sexual activity.

QUESTIONER: In a transition from third to fourth density, we have two other possibilities other than the type that we are experiencing now. We have the possibility of a totally positively polarized harvest and the possibility of a totally negatively polarized harvest that I understand have occurred elsewhere in the universe many times. When there is a totally negatively polarized harvest, the whole planet that has negatively polarized makes the transition from third to fourth density. Does the planet have the experience of the distortion of disease that this planet now experiences prior to that transition?

RA: I am Ra. You are perceptive. The negative harvest is one of intense disharmony, and the planet will express this.

QUESTIONER: The planet has a certain set of conditions in late third density, and then the conditions are different in early fourth density. Could you give me an example of a negatively polarized planet and the conditions in late third density and early fourth density so that I can see how they change?

RA: I am Ra. The vibrations from third to fourth density change on a negatively oriented planet precisely as they do upon a positively oriented planet. With fourth-density negative comes many abilities and possibilities of which you are familiar. The fourth density is more dense, and it is far more difficult to hide the true vibrations of the mind/body/spirit complex. This enables fourth-density negatives, as well as positives, the chance to form social memory complexes. It enables negatively oriented entities the opportunity for a different set of parameters with which to show their power over others and to be of service to the self. The conditions are the same as far as the vibrations are concerned.

QUESTIONER: I was concerned about the amount of physical distortions, disease, and that sort of thing in third-density negative just before harvesting, and in fourth-density negative just after harvesting or in transition. What are the conditions of the physical problems, disease, etc. in late third-density negative?

RA: I am Ra. Each planetary experience is unique. The problems, shall we say, of bellicose actions are more likely to be of pressing concern to late third-density negative entities than the Earth's reactions to negativity of the planetary mind, for it is often by such warlike attitudes on a global scale that the necessary negative polarization is achieved.

As fourth density occurs, there is a new planet and new physical vehicle system gradually expressing itself, and the parameters of bellicose actions become those of thought rather than manifested weapons.

QUESTIONER: Well, then, is physical disease and illness as we know it on this planet rather widespread on a third-density negative planet before harvest into fourth-density negative?

RA: I am Ra. Physical complex distortions of which you speak are likely to be less found as fourth-density negative begins to be a probable choice of harvest due to the extreme interest in the self which characterizes the harvestable third-density negative entity. Much more care is taken of the physical body, as well as much more discipline being offered to the self mentally. This is an orientation of great self-interest and self-discipline. There are still instances of the types of disease which are associated with the mind complex distortions of negative emotions such as anger. However, in a harvestable entity these emotional distortions are much more likely to be used as catalyst in an expressive and destructive sense as regards the object of anger.

QUESTIONER: I am trying to understand the way that disease and bodily distortions are generated with respect to polarities, both positive and negative. It seems that they are generated in some way to create the split of polarization, that they have a function in creating the original polarization that occurs in third density. Is this correct?

RA: I am Ra. This is not precisely correct. Distortions of the bodily or mental complex are those distortions found in beings which have need of experiences which aid in polarization. These polarizations may be those of entities which have already chosen the path or polarization to be followed.

It is more likely for positively oriented individuals to be experiencing distortions within the physical complex due to the lack of consuming interest in the self and the emphasis on service to others. Moreover, in an unpolarized entity, catalyst of the physical distortion nature will be generated at random. The hopeful result is, as you say, the original choice of polarity. Oftentimes this choice is not made but the catalyst continues to be generated. In the negatively oriented individual, the physical body is likely to be more carefully tended and the mind disciplined against physical distortion.

QUESTIONER: This planet, to me, seems to be what I would call a cesspool of distortions. This includes all diseases and malfunctions of the physical body in general. It would seem to me that, on the average, this planet would be very, very high on the list if we just took the overall amount of these problems. Am I correct in this assumption?

RA: I am Ra. We will review previous material.
Catalyst is offered to the entity. If it is not used by the mind

complex, it will then filter through to the body complex and manifest as some form of physical distortion. The more efficient the use of catalyst, the less physical distortion to be found.

There are, in the case of those you call Wanderers, not only a congenital difficulty in dealing with the third-density vibratory patterns but also a recollection, however dim, that these distortions are not necessary or usual in the home vibration.

We overgeneralize as always, for there are many cases of pre-incarnative decisions which result in physical or mental limitations and distortions, but we feel that you are addressing the question of widespread distortions towards misery of one form or another. Indeed, on some third-density planetary spheres, catalyst has been used more efficiently. In the case of your planetary sphere, there is much inefficient use of catalyst and, therefore, much physical distortion.

We have enough energy available for one query at this time.

QUESTIONER: Then I will ask if there is anything that we can do to make the instrument more comfortable or to improve the contact?

RA: I am Ra. Continue as always in love. All is well. You are conscientious.

I am Ra. I leave you in the love and in the light of the One Infinite Creator. Go forth rejoicing in the power and the peace of the One Infinite Creator. Adonai.

Session 67,
August 15, 1981

RA: I am Ra and I greet you in the love and in the light of the One Infinite Creator. I communicate now.

QUESTIONER: Could you first give us the instrument's condition, please?

RA: I am Ra. The vital energies are more closely aligned with the amount of distortion normal to this entity than previous asking showed. The physical complex energy levels are somewhat less strong than at the previous asking. The psychic attack component is exceptionally strong at this particular nexus.

QUESTIONER: Can you describe what you call the psychic attack component, and tell me why it is strong at this particular time?

RA: I am Ra. We shall elect not to retrace previously given information but rather elect to note that the psychic attack upon this instrument is at a constant level as long as it continues in this particular service.

Variations towards the distortion of intensity of attack occur due to the opportunities presented by the entity in any weakness. At this particular nexus the entity has been dealing with the distortion which you call pain for some time, as you call this measurement, and this has a cumulatively weakening effect upon physical energy levels. This creates a particularly favorable target of opportunity, and the entity of which we have previously spoken has taken this opportunity to attempt to be of service in its own way. It is fortunate for the ongoing vitality of this contact that the instrument is a strong-willed entity with little tendency towards the distortion, called among your peoples hysteria, since the dizzying effects of this attack have been constant and at times disruptive for several of your diurnal periods.

However, this particular entity is adapting well to the situation without undue distortions towards fear. Thus the psychic attack is not successful but does have some draining influence upon the instrument.

QUESTIONER: I will ask if I am correct in this analysis. We would consider that the entity making this so-called attack is offering its service with respect to its distortion in our polarized condition now so that we may more fully appreciate its polarity, and we are appreciative of the fact and thank this entity for its attempt to serve our One Creator in bringing to us knowledge in, shall I say, a more complete sense. Is this correct?

RA: I am Ra. There is no correctness or incorrectness to your statement. It is an expression of a positively polarized and balanced view of negatively polarized actions which has the effect of debilitating the strength of the negatively polarized actions.

QUESTIONER: We would welcome the services of the entity who uses, and I will use the misnomer "attack," since I do not consider this an attack but an offering of service, and we welcome this offering of service, but we would be able, I believe, to make more full use of the services if they were not physically disabling the instrument in a minor way. For with a greater physical ability she would be able to more appreciate the service. We would greatly appreciate it if the service was carried on in some manner which we could welcome in even greater love than at present. This, I assume, would be some service that would not include the dizzying effect.

I am trying to understand the mechanism of this service of the entity that seems to be constantly with us, and I am trying to understand the origin of this entity and his mechanism of greeting us. I will make a statement that will probably be incorrect but is a function of my extreme limitation in understanding the other densities and how they work. I am guessing that this particular entity is a member of the Orion Confederation and is possibly incarnate in a body of the appropriate density, which I assume is the fifth, and by mental discipline he has been able to project a portion or all of his consciousness to our coordinates, you might say, here, and it is possibly one of the seven bodies that make up his mind/body/spirit complex. Is any of this correct, and can you tell me what is correct or incorrect about this statement?

RA: I am Ra. The statement is substantially correct.

QUESTIONER: Would you rather not give me information as to the specifics of my statement?

RA: I am Ra. We did not perceive a query in further detail. Please requestion.

QUESTIONER: Which body in respect to the colors does the entity use to travel to us?

RA: I am Ra. This query is not particularly simple to answer due to the transdimensional nature, not only of space/time to time/space but from density to density. The time/space light or fifth-density body is used while the space/time fifth-density body remains in fifth density. The assumption that the consciousness is projected thereby is correct. The assumption that this conscious vehicle attached to the space/time fifth-density physical complex is that vehicle which works in this particular service is correct.

QUESTIONER: I undoubtedly will ask several uninformed questions. However, I was trying to understand certain concepts that have to do with the illusion, I shall say, of polarization that seems to exist at certain density levels in the creation and how the mechanism of the interaction of consciousness works. It seems to me that the fifth-density entity is attracted in some way to our group by the polarization of this group, which acts somehow as a beacon to this entity. Am I correct?

RA: I am Ra. This is, in substance, correct, but the efforts of this entity are put forward only reluctantly. The usual attempts upon positively oriented entities or groups of entities are made, as we have said, by minions of the fifth-density Orion leaders; these are fourth density. The normal gambit of such fourth-density attack is the tempting of the entity or group of entities away from total polarization towards service to others and toward the aggrandizement of self or of social organizations with which the self identifies. In the case of this particular group, each was given a full range of temptations to cease being of service to each other and to the One Infinite Creator. Each entity declined these choices and instead continued with no significant deviation from the desire for a purely other-self service orientation. At this point one of the fifth-density entities overseeing such detuning processes determined that it would be necessary to terminate the group by what you might call magical means, as you understand ritual magic. We have previously discussed the potential for the removal of one of this group by such attack and have noted that by far the most vulnerable is the instrument due to its pre-incarnative physical complex distortions.

QUESTIONER: In order for this group to remain fully in service to the Creator, since we recognize this fifth-density entity as the Creator, we must also attempt to serve in any way we can, this entity. Is it possible for you to communicate to us the desires of this entity if there are any in addition to us simply ceasing the reception and dissemination of that which you provide?

RA: I am Ra. This entity has two desires. The first and foremost is to, shall we say, misplace one or more of this group in a negative orientation so that it may choose to be of service along the path of service to self. The objective which must precede this is the termination of the physical complex viability of one of this group while the mind/body/spirit complex is within a controllable configuration. May we say that although we of Ra have limited understanding, it is our belief that sending this entity love and light, which each of the group is doing, is the most helpful catalyst which the group may offer to this entity.

QUESTIONER: We find a—I'm sorry. Please continue.

RA: I am Ra. We were about to note that this entity has been as neutralized as possible in our estimation by this love offering, and thus its continued presence is perhaps the understandable limit for each polarity of the various views of service which each may render to the other.

QUESTIONER: We have a paradoxical situation with respect to serving the Creator. We have requests, from those whom we serve in this density, for Ra's information. However, we have requests from another density not to disseminate this information. We have portions of the Creator requesting two seemingly opposite activities of this group. It would be very helpful if we could reach the condition of full service in such a way that we were by every thought and activity serving the Creator to the very best of our ability. Is it possible for you to solve, or for the fifth-density entity who offers its service to solve, this paradox which I have observed?

RA: I am Ra. It is quite possible.

QUESTIONER: Then how could we solve this paradox?

RA: I am Ra. Consider, if you will, that you have no ability not to serve the Creator since all is the Creator. You do not have merely two opposite requests for information or lack of information from this source if you listen carefully to those whose voices you may hear. This is all one voice to which you resonate upon a certain frequency. This frequency determines your choice of service to the One Creator. As it happens, this group's vibratory patterns and those of Ra are compatible and enable us to speak through this instrument with your support. This is a function of free will.

A portion, seemingly of the Creator, rejoices at your choice to question us regarding the evolution of spirit. A seemingly separate portion would wish for multitudinous answers to a great range of queries of a specific nature. Another seemingly separate group of your peoples would wish this correspondence through this instrument to cease, feeling it to be of a negative nature. Upon the many other planes of existence, there are those whose every fiber rejoices at your service, and those such as the entity of whom you have been speaking which wish only to terminate the life upon the third-density plane of this instrument. All are the Creator. There is one vast panoply of biases and distortions, colors and hues, in an unending pattern. In the case of those with whom you, as entities and as a group, are not in resonance, you wish them love, light, peace, joy, and bid them well. No more than this can you do for your portion of the Creator is as it is, and your experience and offering of experience, to be valuable, needs be more and more a perfect representation of who you truly are. Could you, then, serve a negative entity by offering the instrument's life? It is unlikely that you would find this a true service. Thus you may see in many cases the loving balance being achieved, the love being offered, light being sent, and the service of the service-to-self-oriented entity gratefully acknowledged while being rejected as not being useful in your journey at this time. Thus you serve One Creator without paradox.

QUESTIONER: This particular entity, by his service, is able to create a dizzying effect on the instrument. Could you describe the mechanics of such a service?

RA: I am Ra. This instrument, in the small times of its incarnation, had the distortion in the area of the otic complex of many infections, which caused great difficulties at this small age, as you would call it. The scars of these distortions remain, and indeed that which you call the sinus system remains distorted. Thus the entity works with these distortions to produce a loss of the balance and a slight lack of ability to use the optic apparatus.

QUESTIONER: I was wondering about the magical, shall I say, principles used by the fifth-density entity giving this service and his ability to give it. Why is he able to utilize these particular physical distortions from the philosophical or magical point of view?

RA: I am Ra. This entity is able to, shall we say, penetrate in time/space configuration the field of this particular entity. It has moved through the quarantine without any vehicle and thus has been more able to escape detection by the net of the Guardians.

This is the great virtue of the magical working whereby consciousness is sent forth essentially without vehicle as light. The light would work instantly upon an untuned individual by suggestion; that is, the stepping out in front of the traffic because the suggestion is that there is no traffic. This entity, as each in this group, is enough disciplined in the ways of love and light that it is not suggestible to any great extent. However, there is a predisposition of the physical complex which this entity is making maximal use of as regards the instrument, hoping, for instance, by means of increasing dizziness to cause the instrument to fall or to indeed walk in front of your traffic because of impaired vision.

The magical principles, shall we say, may be loosely translated into your system of magic, whereby symbols are used and traced and visualized in order to develop the power of the light.

QUESTIONER: Do you mean then that this fifth-density entity visualizes certain symbols? I am assuming that these symbols are of a nature where their continued use would have some power or charge. Am I correct?

RA: I am Ra. You are correct. In fifth density, light is as visible a tool as your pencil's writing.

QUESTIONER: Then am I correct in assuming that this entity configures the light into symbology; that is, what we would call a physical presence? Is this correct?

RA: I am Ra. This is incorrect. The light is used to create a sufficient purity of environment for the entity to place its consciousness in a carefully created light vehicle which then uses the tools of light to do its working. The will and presence are those of the entity doing the working.

QUESTIONER: The fifth-density entity you mentioned penetrated the quarantine. Was this done through one of the windows or was this because of his, shall I say, magical ability?

RA: I am Ra. This was done through a very slight window which less magically oriented entities or groups could not have used to advantage.

QUESTIONER: The main point with this line of questioning has to do with the first distortion and the fact that this window exists. Was this a portion of the random effect, and are we experiencing the same type of balancing in receiving the offerings of this entity as the planet in general receives because of the window effect?

RA: I am Ra. This is precisely correct. As the planetary sphere accepts more highly evolved positive entities or groups with information to offer, the same opportunity must be offered to similarly wise negatively oriented entities or groups.

QUESTIONER: Then we experience in this seeming difficulty the wisdom of the first distortion and for that reason must fully accept that which we experience. This is my personal view. Is it congruent with Ra's?

RA: I am Ra. In our view we would perhaps go further in expressing appreciation of this opportunity. This is an intensive opportunity in that it is quite marked in its effects, both actual and potential, and as it affects the instrument's distortions towards pain and other difficulties such as the dizziness, it enables the instrument to continuously choose to serve others and to serve the Creator.

Similarly it offers a continual opportunity for each in the group to express support under more distorted or difficult circumstances of the other-self experiencing the brunt, shall we say, of this attack, thus being able to demonstrate the love and light of the Infinite Creator and, furthermore, choosing working by working to continue to serve as messengers for this information which we attempt to offer and to serve the Creator thereby.

Thus the opportunities are quite noticeable, as well as the distortions caused by this circumstance.

QUESTIONER: Thank you. Is this so-called attack offered to myself and [name] as well as the instrument?

RA: I am Ra. This is correct.

QUESTIONER: I personally have felt no effect that I am aware of. Is it possible for you to tell me how we are offered this service?

RA: I am Ra. The questioner has been offered the service of doubting the self and of becoming disheartened over various distortions of the personal nature. This entity has not chosen to use these opportunities, and the Orion entity has basically ceased to be interested in maintaining constant surveillance of this entity.

The scribe is under constant surveillance and has been offered numerous opportunities for the intensification of the mental/emotional distortions and in some cases the connection matrices between mental/emotional complexes and the physical complex counterpart. As this entity has become aware of these attacks, it has become much less pervious to them. This is the particular cause of the great intensification and constancy of the surveillance of the instrument, for it is the weak link due to factors beyond its control within this incarnation.

QUESTIONER: Is it within the first distortion to tell me why the instrument experienced so many physical distortions during the new times of its physical incarnation?

RA: I am Ra. This is correct.

QUESTIONER: In that case, can you answer me as to why the instrument experienced so much during its early years?

RA: I am Ra. We were affirming the correctness of your assumption that such answers would be breaking the Way of Confusion. It is not appropriate for such answers to be laid out as a table spread for dinner. It is appropriate that the complexes of opportunity involved be contemplated.

QUESTIONER: Then there is no other service at this time that we can offer that fifth-density entity of the Orion group who is constantly with us. As I see it now from your point of view, there is nothing that we can do for him? Is this correct?

RA: I am Ra. This is correct. There is great humor in your attempt to be of polarized service to the opposite polarity. There is a natural difficulty in doing so, since what you consider service is considered by this entity nonservice. As you send this entity love and light and wish it well, it loses its polarity and needs to regroup.

Thus it would not consider your service as such. On the other hand, if you allowed it to be of service by removing this instrument from your midst, you might perhaps perceive this as not being of service. You have here a balanced and polarized view of the Creator; two services offered, mutually rejected, and in a state of equilibrium in which free will is preserved and each allowed to go upon its own path of experiencing the One Infinite Creator.

QUESTIONER: Thank you. In closing that part of the discussion I would just say that if there is anything that we can do that is within our ability—and I understand that there are many things such as the ones that you just mentioned that are not within our ability—that we could do for this particular entity, if you would in the future communicate its requests to us, we will at least consider them because we would like to serve in every respect. Is this agreeable to you?

RA: I am Ra. We perceive that we have not been able to clarify your service versus its desire for service. You need, in our humble opinion, to look at the humor of the situation and relinquish your desire to serve where no service is requested. The magnet will attract or repel. Glory in the strength of your polarization and allow others of opposite polarity to similarly do so, seeing the great humor of this polarity and its complications in view of the unification in sixth density of these two paths.

QUESTIONER: Thank you very much. I have a statement here that I will have you comment on for accuracy or inaccuracy. In general, the archetypical mind is a representation of facets of the One Infinite Creation. The Father archetype corresponds to the male or positive aspect of electromagnetic energy and is active, creative, and radiant, as is our local sun. The Mother archetype corresponds to the female or negative aspect of electromagnetic energy and is receptive or magnetic, as is our Earth as it receives the sun's rays and brings forth life via third-density fertility. The Prodigal Son or the Fool archetype corresponds to every entity who seems to have strayed from unity and seeks to return to the One Infinite Creator. The Devil archetype represents the illusion of the material world and the appearance of evil but is more accurately the provider of catalyst for the growth of each entity within the third-density illusion. The Magician, Saint, Healer, or Adept corresponds to the Higher Self and, because of the balance within its energy centers, pierces the illusion to contact intelligent infinity and thereby demonstrates mastery of the catalyst of third density. The archetype of Death symbolizes the transition of an entity from the yellow-ray body to the green-ray body either temporarily between incarnations or, more permanently, at harvest.

Each archetype presents an aspect of the One Infinite Creation to teach the individual mind/body/spirit complex according to the calling or the electromagnetic configuration of mind of the entity. Teaching is done via the intuition. With the proper seeking or mind configuration, the power of will uses the spirit as a shuttle to contact the appropriate archetypical aspect necessary for the teach/learning. In the same way, each of the other informers of intuition are contacted. They are hierarchical and proceed from the entity's own subconscious mind, to group or planetary mind, to guides, to Higher Self, to archetypical mind, to cosmic mind or intelligent infinity. Each is contacted by the spirit, serving as shuttle according to the harmonized electromagnetic configuration of the seeker's mind and the information sought.

Would you please comment on the accuracy of these observations and correct any errors and fill in any omissions?

RA: I am Ra. The entity has been using transferred energy for most of this session due to its depleted physical levels. We shall begin this rather complex answer, which is interesting, but do not expect to finish it. Those portions which we do not respond to we ask that you requestion us on at a working in your future.

QUESTIONER: Perhaps it would be better to start the next session with the answer to this question. Would that be appropriate, or is the energy already fixed?

RA: I am Ra. The energy is as always allotted. The choice, as always, is yours.

QUESTIONER: In that case, continue.

RA: I am Ra. Perhaps the first item we shall address is the concept of the spirit used as a shuttle between the roots and the trunk of mind. This is a misapprehension, and we shall allow the questioner to consider the function of the spirit further, for in working with the mind we are working within one complex and have not yet attempted to penetrate intelligent infinity. It is well said that archetypes are portions of the One Infinite Creator or aspects of its face. It is, however, far better to realize that the archetypes, while constant in the complex of generative energies offered, do not give the same yield of these complexes to any two seekers. Each seeker will experience each archetype in the characteristics within the complex of the archetype which are most important to it. An example of this would be the observation of the questioner that the Fool is described in such and such a way. One great aspect of this archetype is the aspect of faith, the walking into space without regard for what is to come next. This is, of course, foolish but is part of the characteristic of the spiritual neophyte. That this aspect was not seen may be pondered by the questioner. At this time we shall again request that the query be restated at the next working, and we shall at this time cease using this instrument. Before we leave, may we ask if there may be any short questions?

QUESTIONER: Only if there is anything that we can do to make the instrument more comfortable or to improve the contact?

RA: I am Ra. Continue, my friends, in the strength of harmony, love, and light. All is well. The alignments are appreciated for their careful placement.

I am Ra. I leave you now, my friends, in the glory of the love and the light of the Infinite Creator. Go forth, then, rejoicing in the power and the peace of the One Infinite Creator. Adonai.

Session 68,
August 18, 1981

RA: I am Ra. I greet you in the love and in the light of the One Infinite Creator. We communicate now.

QUESTIONER: The primary reason that we decided to have this session today is that I might not be around for a while, and I had a pressing question about what happened Sunday night when, apparently, the instrument was slipping into a trance state during one of the normal Sunday night meditations, and I would like to question you on this. Can you give me information about what happened?

RA: I am Ra. We can.

QUESTIONER: Would you tell me what happened in that case?

RA: I am Ra. We have instructed this instrument to refrain from calling us unless it is within this set of circumscribed circumstances. In the event of which you speak, this instrument was asked a question which pertained to what you have been calling the Ra Material. This instrument was providing the voice for our brothers and sisters of the wisdom density known to you as Latwii.

This instrument thought to itself, "I do not know this answer. I wish I were channeling Ra." The ones of Latwii found themselves in the position of being approached by the Orion entity which seeks to be of service in its own way. The instrument began to prepare for Ra contact. Latwii knew that if this was completed, the Orion entity would have an opportunity which Latwii wished to avoid.

It is fortunate for this instrument, firstly, that Latwii is of fifth density and able to deal with that particular vibratory complex which the Orion entity was manifesting and, secondly, that there were those in the support group at that time which sent great amounts of support to the instrument in this crux. Thus what occurred was the ones of Latwii never let go of this instrument, although this came perilously close to breaking the Way of Confusion. It continued to hold its connection with the mind/body/spirit complex of the instrument and to generate information through it even as the instrument began to slip out of its physical vehicle.

The act of continued communication caused the entity to be unable to grasp the instrument's mind/body/spirit complex, and after but a small measure of your space/time, Latwii recovered the now completely amalgamated instrument and gave it continued communication to steady it during the transition back into integration.

QUESTIONER: Could you tell me what the plan of the fifth-density negatively oriented entity was, and how it would have accomplished it and what the results would have been if it had worked?

RA: I am Ra. The plan, which is ongoing, was to take the mind/body/spirit complex while it was separated from its yellow body physical complex shell, to then place this mind/body/spirit complex within the negative portions of your time/space. The shell would then become that of the unknowing, unconscious entity and could be, shall we say, worked upon to cause malfunction which would end in coma and then in what you call the death of the body. At this point the Higher Self of the instrument would have the choice of leaving the mind/body/spirit complex in negative sp—we correct—time/space or of allowing incarnation in space/time of equivalent vibration and polarity distortions. Thus this entity would become a negatively polarized entity without the advantage of native negative polarization. It would find a long path to the Creator under these circumstances, although the path would inevitably end well.

QUESTIONER: Then you are saying that if this fifth-density negative entity is successful in its attempts to transfer the mind/body/spirit complex when that complex is in what we call the trance state to negatively polarized time/space, then the Higher Self has no choice but to allow incarnation in negatively polarized space/time? Is that correct?

RA: I am Ra. This is incorrect. The Higher Self could allow the mind/body/spirit complex to remain in time/space. However, it is unlikely that the Higher Self would do so indefinitely, due to its distortion towards the belief that the function of the mind/body/spirit complex is to experience and learn from other-selves, thus experiencing the Creator. A highly polarized positive mind/body/spirit complex surrounded by negative portions of space/time will experience only darkness, for like the magnet, there is no, shall we say, likeness. Thus a barrier is automatically formed.

QUESTIONER: Let me be sure that I understand you. Is that darkness experienced in negative space/time or in negative time/space?

RA: I am Ra. Negative time/space.

QUESTIONER: Incarnation in negative space/time then in a condition like that would result in incarnation into which density level for, let us take as an example, the instrument?

RA: I am Ra. The answer to this query violates the first distortion.

QUESTIONER: OK, then, let's not take the instrument as an example. Let's assume that this was done to a Wanderer of sixth density. If this answer violates the first distortion, don't answer. But let's say a sixth-density Wanderer had this happen and went into negative time/space. Would that be a sixth-density negative time/space, and would he incarnate into sixth-density negative space/time?

RA: I am Ra. Your assumption is correct. The strength of the polarization would be matched as far as possible. In some positive sixth-density Wanderers, the approximation would not quite be complete due to the paucity of negative sixth-density energy fields of the equivalent strength.

QUESTIONER: Is the reason that this could be done the fact that the Wanderer's mind/body/spirit complex extracted in what we call the trance state, leaving the third-density physical; in this state the Wanderer does not have the full capability to magically defend itself. Is this correct?

RA: I am Ra. In the case of this instrument, this is correct. This is also correct when applied almost without exception to those instruments working in trance which have not consciously experienced magical training in time/space in the, shall we say, present incarnation. The entities of your density capable of magical defense in this situation are extremely rare.

QUESTIONER: It would seem to me that since I can't imagine anything worse than this particular result, it would be very advisable to seek the magical training and defense for this situation. Could Ra and would Ra instruct us in this type of magical defense?

RA: I am Ra. This request lies beyond the first distortion. The entity seeking magical ability must do so in a certain manner. We may give instructions of a general nature. This we have already done. The instrument has begun the process of balancing the self. This is a lengthy process.

To take an entity before it is ready and offer it the scepter of magical power is to infringe in an unbalanced manner. We may suggest with some asperity that the instrument never call upon Ra in any way while unprotected by the configuration which is at this time present.

QUESTIONER: I think that it is important for me to investigate the techniques, if they are within the first distortion, of the fifth-density entity who wishes to displace the mind/body/spirit complexes of this group. Am I within the first distortion in asking you to describe how this entity goes about this working?

RA: I am Ra. You are.

QUESTIONER: Well, then, how does this fifth-density entity go about this working from the very start of being alerted to the fact that we exist?

RA: I am Ra. The entity becomes aware of power. This power has the capacity of energizing those which may be available for harvest. This entity is desirous of disabling this power source. It sends its legions. Temptations are offered. They are ignored or rejected. The power source persists and indeed improves its inner connections of harmony and love of service.

The entity determines that it must needs attempt the disabling itself. By means of projection it enters the vicinity of this power source. It assesses the situation. It is bound by the first distortion but may take advantage of any free-will distortion. The free-will, pre-incarnative distortions of the instrument with regard to the physical vehicle seem the most promising target. Any distortion away from service to others is also appropriate.

When the instrument leaves its physical vehicle, it does so freely. Thus the misplacement of the mind/body/spirit complex of the instrument would not be a violation of its free will if it followed the entity freely. This is the process.

We are aware of your pressing desire to know how to become impervious as a group to any influences such as this. The processes which you seek are a matter of your free choice. You are aware of the principles of magical work. We cannot speak to advise but can only suggest, as we have before, that it would be appropriate for this group to embark upon such a path as a group, but not individually, for obvious reasons.

QUESTIONER: I am interested as to how the first distortion applies to the negatively polarized entity misplacing the mind/body/spirit complex. Why is the negatively polarized entity followed to the place of negative time/space? Why would one of us freely follow the entity?

RA: I am Ra. The positive polarity sees love in all things. The negative polarity is clever.

QUESTIONER: Then I am assuming if the negative polarity used any other approach that did not use the free will of the other-self, he would lose polarization and magical power. This is correct, isn't it?

RA: I am Ra. This is correct. The transferred energy grows low. We wish to close. Are there any short queries before we leave this instrument?

QUESTIONER: Only if there is anything that we can do to make the instrument more comfortable or to improve the contact?

RA: I am Ra. You are conscientious. We realize your necessity for these queries. All is well, my friends. We thank you and leave you in the love and in the light of the One Infinite Creator. Go forth, therefore, rejoicing in the power and in the peace of the One Infinite Creator. Adonai.

Session 69,
August 29, 1981

RA: I am Ra; I greet you in the love and in the light of the One Infinite Creator.
    Before we proceed, may we make a small request for future workings. At this particular working there is some slight interference with the contact due to the hair of the instrument. We may suggest the combing of this antenna-like material into a more orderly configuration prior to the working.
    We communicate now.

QUESTIONER: A question which I didn't get to ask at the previous session and which I will be forced to ask at this time is, Is the trance state the only state in which a mind/body/spirit positive entity may be lured by a negative entity or adept to negative time/space configuration?

RA: I am Ra. This is a misperceived concept. The mind/body/spirit complex which freely leaves the third-density physical complex is vulnerable when the appropriate protection is not at hand. You may perceive carefully that very few entities which choose to leave their physical complexes are doing work of such a nature as to attract the polarized attention of negatively oriented entities. The danger to most in trance state, as you term the physical complex being left, is the touching of the physical complex in such a manner as to attract the mind/body/spirit complex back thereunto or to damage the means by which that which you call ectoplasm is being recalled. This instrument is an anomaly in that it is well that the instrument not be touched or artificial light thrown upon it while in the trance state. However, the ectoplasmic activity is interiorized. The main difficulty, as you are aware, is then the previously discussed negative removal of the entity under its free will.

That this can happen only in the trance state is not completely certain, but it is highly probable that in another out-of-body experience such as death, the entity here examined would, as most positively polarized entities, have a great deal of protection from comrades, guides, and portions of the self which would be aware of the transfer you call the physical death.

QUESTIONER: Then you are saying that the protective friends, we will call them, would be available in every condition except for what we call the trance state, which seems to be anomalistic with respect to the others. Is this correct?

RA: I am Ra. This is correct.

QUESTIONER: Why is this trance state, as we call it, different? Why are there not entities available in this particular state?

RA: I am Ra. The uniqueness of this situation is not the lack of friends, for this, as all entities, has its guides or angelic presences and, due to polarization, teachers and friends also. The unique characteristic of the workings which the social memory complex Ra and your group have begun is the intent to serve others with the highest attempt at near purity which we as comrades may achieve.

This has alerted a much more determined friend of negative polarity which is interested in removing this particular opportunity.

We may say once again two notes: Firstly, we searched long to find an appropriate channel or instrument and an appropriate support group. If this opportunity is ended, we shall be grateful for that which has been done, but the possibility/probability vortices indicating the location of this configuration again are slight. Secondly, we thank you for we know what you sacrifice in order to do that which you as a group wish to do.

We will not deplete this instrument insofar as we are able. We have attempted to speak of how the instrument may deplete itself through too great a dedication to the working. All these things and all else we have said has been heard. We are thankful. In the present situation we express thanks to the entities who call themselves Latwii.

QUESTIONER: Do I understand, then, that death, whether it is by natural means or accidental means or suicide, that all deaths of this type would create the same after-death condition that would avail the entity to its protection from friends? Is this correct?

RA: I am Ra. We presume you mean to inquire whether in the death experience, no matter what the cause, the negative friends are not able to remove an entity. This is correct largely because the entity without the attachment to the space/time physical complex is far more aware and without the gullibility which is somewhat the hallmark of those who love wholeheartedly.

However, the death, if natural, would undoubtedly be the more harmonious; the death by murder being confused and the entity needing some time/space in which to get its bearings, so to speak; the death by suicide causing the necessity for much healing work and, shall we say, the making of a dedication to the third density for the renewed opportunity of learning the lessons set by the Higher Self.

QUESTIONER: Is this also true of unconscious conditions due to accident, or medical anesthetic, or drugs?

RA: I am Ra. Given that the entity is not attempting to be of service in this particular way which is proceeding now, the entities of negative orientation would not find it possible to remove the mind/body/spirit. The unique characteristic, as we have said, which is, shall we say, dangerous is the willing of the mind/body/spirit complex outward from the physical complex of third density for the purpose of service-to-others. In any other situation this circumstance would not be in effect.

QUESTIONER: Would this be a function of the balancing action of the first distortion?

RA: I am Ra. Your query is somewhat opaque. Please restate for specificity.

QUESTIONER: I was just guessing that since the mind/body/spirit complex's will from the third-density body for a particular duty or service to others would then create a situation primarily with respect to the first distortion where the opportunity for balancing this service by the negative service would be available and, therefore, magically possible for the intrusion of the other polarization. Is this thinking at all correct?

RA: I am Ra. No. The free will of the instrument is indeed a necessary part of the opportunity afforded the Orion group. However, this free will and the first distortion applies only to the instrument. The entire hope of the Orion group is to infringe upon free will without losing polarity. Thus this group, if represented by a wise entity, attempts to be clever.

QUESTIONER: Has a Wanderer ever been so infringed upon by a negative adept and then placed in negative time/space?

RA: I am Ra. This is correct.

QUESTIONER: Can you tell me the situation that the Wanderer finds himself in and the path back, why that path could not be the simple moving back into positive time/space?

RA: I am Ra. The path back revolves, firstly, about the Higher Self's reluctance to enter negative space/time. This may be a significant part of the length of that path. Secondly, when a positively oriented entity incarnates in a thoroughly negative environment, it must needs learn/ teach the lessons of the love of self, thus becoming one with its other-selves.

When this has been accomplished, the entity may then choose to release the potential difference and change polarities. However, the process of learning the accumulated lessons of love of self may be quite lengthy. Also the entity, in learning these lessons, may lose much positive orientation during the process, and the choice of reversing polarities may be delayed until the mid-sixth density. All of this is, in your way of measurement, time consuming, although the end result is well.

QUESTIONER: Is it possible to tell me roughly how many Wanderers who have come to this planet during this master cycle have experienced this displacement into a negative time/space?

RA: I am Ra. We can note the number of such occurrences. There has been only one. We cannot, due to the Law of Confusion, discuss the entity.

QUESTIONER: You said that the Higher Self is reluctant to enter negative space/time. Is that correct?

RA: I am Ra. The incarnative process involves being incarnated from time/space to space/time. This is correct.

QUESTIONER: I will make this statement and see if I am correct. When first moved into time/space of a negative polarization, the positive entity experiences nothing but darkness. Then, by incarnation into negative space/time by the Higher Self, it experiences a negative space/time environment with negatively polarized other-selves. Is this correct?

RA: I am Ra. This is correct.

QUESTIONER: It would seem to me that it would be an extremely difficult situation for the positively polarized entity, and the learning process would be extremely traumatic. Is this correct?

RA: I am Ra. Let us say that the positively polarized individual makes a poor student of the love of self and thus spends much more time, if you will, than those native to that pattern of vibrations.

QUESTIONER: I am assuming that this misplacement must be a function of his free will in some way. Is this correct?

RA: I am Ra. This is absolutely correct.

QUESTIONER: This is a point that I find quite confusing to me. It is the function of the free will of the positively oriented entity to move into the negatively polarized time/space. However, it is also a function of his lack of understanding of what he is doing. I am sure that if the entity had full understanding of what he was doing, he would not do it. It is a function of his negatively polarized other-self creating a situation where he is lured to that configuration. What is the principle with respect to the first distortion that allows this to occur, since we have two portions of the Creator, each of equal value or of equal potential but oppositely polarized, and we have this situation resulting. Could you tell me the philosophical principle behind this particular act?

RA: I am Ra. There are two important points in this regard. Firstly, we may note the situation wherein an entity gets a road map which is poorly marked and in fact is quite incorrect. The entity sets out to its destination. It wishes only to reach the point of destination, but, becoming confused by the faulty authority and not knowing the territory through which it drives, it becomes hopelessly lost.

Free will does not mean that there will be no circumstances when calculations will be awry. This is so in all aspects of the life experience. Although there are no mistakes, there are surprises.

Secondly, that which we and you do in workings such as this carries a magical charge, if you would use this much misunderstood term; perhaps we may say a metaphysical power. Those who do work of power are available for communication to and from entities of roughly similar power. It is fortunate that the Orion entity does not have the native power of this group. However, it is quite disciplined, whereas this group lacks the finesse equivalent to its power. Each is working in consciousness, but the group has not begun a work as a group. The individual work is helpful, for the group is mutually an aid, one to another.

QUESTIONER: This instrument performs services that involve channeling other members of the Confederation. We are reluctant to continue this because of the possibility of her slipping into trance and being offered the services of the negatively polarized entity or adept. Are there any safeguards to create a situation whereby she cannot go into trance other than at a protected working such as this one?

RA: I am Ra. There are three. Firstly, the instrument must needs improve the disciplined subconscious taboo against requesting Ra. This would involve daily conscious and serious thought. The second safeguard is the refraining from the opening of the instrument to questions and answers for the present. The third is quite gross in its appearance but suffices to keep the instrument in its physical complex. The hand may be held.

QUESTIONER: Are you saying, then, that just by holding the instrument's hand during the channeling sessions, this would prevent trance?

RA: I am Ra. This would prevent those levels of meditation which necessarily precede trance. Also in the event that, unlikely as it might seem, the entity grew able to leave the physical complex, the auric infringement and tactile pressure would cause the mind/body/spirit complex to refrain from leaving.

We may note that long practice at the art which each intuits here would be helpful. We cannot speak of methodology, for the infringement would be most great. However, to speak of group efforts is, as we scan each, merely confirmation of what is known. Therefore, this we may do.

We have the available energy for one fairly brief query.

QUESTIONER: There are many techniques and ways of practicing so-called white magical arts. Are rituals designed by a particular group for their own particular use just as good or possibly better than those that have been practiced by groups such as the Order of the Golden Dawn and other magical groups?

RA: I am Ra. Although we are unable to speak with precision on this query, we may note some gratification that the questioner has penetrated some of the gist of a formidable system of service and discipline.

I am Ra. May we thank you again, my friends, for your conscientiousness. All is well. We leave you rejoicing in the power and the peace of the One Infinite Creator. Go forth with joy. Adonai.

Session 70,
September 9, 1981

RA: I am Ra. I greet you in the love and in the light of the One Infinite Creator. We communicate now.

QUESTIONER: Could you please give me an indication of the condition of the instrument?

RA: I am Ra. We are gratified to say that it is as previously stated.

QUESTIONER: Why do you say that you are gratified to say that?

RA: I am Ra. We say this due to a sense of gratitude at the elements which have enabled this instrument to maintain, against great odds, its vital energy at normal vibratory strength. As long as this complex of energies is satisfactory, we may use this instrument without depletion regardless of the distortions previously mentioned.

QUESTIONER: The instrument has complained of intensive psychic attack for the past diurnal period, approximately. Is there a reason for the intensification of this psychic attack?

RA: I am Ra. Yes.

QUESTIONER: Can you tell me what this reason is, please?

RA: I am Ra. The cause is that with which you are intimately involved; that is, the cause is the intensive seeking for what you may call enlightenment. This seeking upon your parts has not abated, but intensified.

In the general case, pain, as you call this distortion and the various exaggerations of this distortion by psychic attack, would, after the depletion of physical complex energy, begin the depletion of vital energy. This instrument guards its vital energy due to previous errors upon its part. Its subconscious will, which is preternaturally strong for this density, has put a ward upon this energy complex. Thus the Orion visitor strives with more and more intensity to disturb this vital energy as this group intensifies its dedication to service through enlightenment.

QUESTIONER: I have an extra little question that I want to throw in at this time. Is regressive hypnosis on an individual past birth in this incarnation, to reveal memories to it of previous incarnations, a service or a disservice to it?

RA: I am Ra. We scan your query and find you shall apply the answer to your future. This causes us to be concerned with the first distortion. However, the query is also general and contains an opportunity for us to express a significant point. Therefore, we shall speak.

There is an infinite range of possibility of service/disservice in the situation of time-regression hypnosis, as you term this means of aiding memory. It has nothing to do with the hypnotist. It has only to do with the use which the entity so hypnotized makes of the information so gleaned. If the hypnotist desires to serve and if such a service is performed only upon sincere request, the hypnotist is attempting to be of service.

QUESTIONER: In the last session, Ra stated that "the path back from sixth-density negative time/space revolves, firstly, about the Higher Self's reluctance to enter negative time/space." Could you explain the Higher Self's position with respect to positive and negative time/space, and why it is so reluctant to enter negative time/space that it is necessary for the mind/body/spirit complex to incarnate in negative space/time to find its path back?

RA: I am Ra. In brief, you have answered your own query. Please question further for more precise information.

QUESTIONER: Why is the Higher Self reluctant to enter negative time/space?

RA: I am Ra. The Higher Self is reluctant to allow its mind/body/spirit complex to enter negative time/space for the same basic reason an entity of your societal complex would be reluctant to enter a prison.

QUESTIONER: What I am trying to understand here is more about the Higher Self and its relationship with the mind/body/spirit complex. Does the Higher Self have a sixth-density mind/body/spirit complex that is a separate unit from the mind/body/spirit complex that is, in this case, displaced to negative time/space?

RA: I am Ra. This is correct. The Higher Self is the entity of mid-sixth density, which, turning back, offers this service to its self.

QUESTIONER: I think I have an erroneous concept of the mind/body/spirit complex that, for instance, I represent here in this density and my Higher Self. This probably comes from my concept of space and time. I am going to try to unscramble this. The way I see it right now is that I am existing in two different locations, here and in mid-sixth density, simultaneously. Is this correct?

RA: I am Ra. You are existing at all levels simultaneously. It is specifically correct that your Higher Self is you in mid-sixth density, and, in your way of measuring what you know of as time, your Higher Self is your self in your future.

QUESTIONER: Am I correct in assuming that all of the mind/body/spirit complexes that exist below levels of mid-sixth density have a Higher Self at the level of mid-sixth density? Is this correct?

RA: I am Ra. This is correct.

QUESTIONER: Would an analogy for this situation be that an individual's Higher Self is manipulating to some extent, shall I say, the mind/body/spirit complex that is its analog to move it through the lower densities for the purposes of gaining experience and finally transferring that experience or amalgamating it in mid-sixth density with the Higher Self?

RA: I am Ra. This is incorrect. The Higher Self does not manipulate its past selves. It protects when possible and guides when asked, but the force of free will is paramount. The seeming contradictions of determinism and free will melt when it is accepted that there is such a thing as true simultaneity. The Higher Self is the end result of all the development experienced by the mind/body/spirit complex to that point.

QUESTIONER: Then what we are looking at is a long path of experience through the densities up to mid-sixth density, which is a function totally of free will and results in the awareness of the Higher Self in mid-sixth density, but since time is illusory and there is a, shall I say, unification of time and space or an eradication of what we think of as time, then all of this experience that results in the Higher Self, the cause of evolution through the densities, is existing while the evolution takes place. It is all simultaneous. Is this correct?

RA: I am Ra. We refrain from speaking of correctness due to our understanding of the immense difficulty of absorbing the concepts of metaphysical existence. In time/space, which is precisely as much of your self as is space/time, all times are simultaneous just as, in your geography, your cities and villages are all functioning, bustling, and alive with entities going about their business at once. So it is in time/space with the self.

QUESTIONER: The Higher Self existing in mid-sixth density seems to be at the point where the negative and positive paths of experience merge into one. Is there a reason for this?

RA: I am Ra. We have covered this material previously.

QUESTIONER: Oh yes. Sorry about that. It slipped my mind. Now, if a positive entity is displaced to negative time/space, I understand that the Higher Self is reluctant to enter the negative time/space. For some reason it makes it necessary for the mind/body/spirit complex to incarnate in negative space/time. Why is it necessary for this incarnation in negative space/time?

RA: I am Ra. Firstly, let us remove the concept of reluctance from the equation and then, secondly, address your query more to the point. Each time/space is an analog of a particular sort or vibration of space/time. When a negative time/space is entered by an entity, the next experience will be that of the appropriate space/time. This is normally done by the form-making body of a mind/body/spirit complex which places the entity in the proper time/space for incarnation.

QUESTIONER: I think that to clear up this point, I will ask a few questions that are related that will possibly help me to understand this better, because I am really confused about this and I think it is a very important point in understanding the creation and the Creator in general, you might say. If a Wanderer of fourth, fifth, or sixth density dies from this third-density state in which we presently find ourselves, does he then find himself in the third-density time/space after death?

RA: I am Ra. This will depend upon the plan which has been approved by the Council of Nine. Some Wanderers offer themselves for but one incarnation, while others offer themselves for varying lengths of your time, up to and including the last two cycles of 25,000 years. If the agreed-upon mission is completed, the Wanderer's mind/body/spirit complex will go to the home vibration.

QUESTIONER: Have there been any Wanderers on this planet for the past 50,000 years now?

RA: I am Ra. There have been a few. There have been many more which chose to join this last cycle of 25,000 years, and many, many more which have come for harvest.

QUESTIONER: Now here is the point of my confusion. If, after physical death, a Wanderer would return to his home planet, why cannot the same entity be extracted from negative time/space to the home planet rather than incarnating in negative space/time?

RA: I am Ra. As we stated, the position in negative time/space, of which we previously were speaking, is that position which is pre-incarnative. After the death of the physical complex in yellow-ray activation, the mind/body/spirit complex moves to a far different portion of time/space in which the indigo body will allow much healing and review to take place before any movement is made towards another incarnative experience.

I perceive a basic miscalculation upon your part, in that time/space is no more homogeneous than space/time. It is as complex and complete a system of illusions, dances, and pattern as is space/time, and has as structured a system of what you may call natural laws.

QUESTIONER: I'll ask this question to inform me a little about what you just stated. When you came to this planet in craft 18,000 and 11,000 years ago, these craft have been called bell craft and were photographed by George Adamski. If I am correct, these craft looked somewhat like a bell; they had portholes around them in the upper portions, and they had three hemispheres at 120° apart underneath. Is this correct?

RA: I am Ra. This is correct.

QUESTIONER: Were these constructed in time/space or in space/time?

RA: I am Ra. We ask your persistent patience, for our answer must be complex.

A construct of thought was formed in time/space. This portion of time/space is that which approaches the speed of light. In time/space, at this approach, the conditions are such that time becomes infinite and mass ceases, so that one which is able to skim the, shall we say, boundary strength of this time/space is able to become placed where it will.

When we were where we wished to be, we then clothed the construct of light with that which would appear as the crystal bell. This was formed through the boundary into space/time. Thus there were two constructs: the time/space or immaterial construct, and the space/time or materialized construct.

QUESTIONER: Was there a reason for the particular shape that you chose, in particular a reason for the three hemispheres on the bottom?

RA: I am Ra. It seemed an aesthetically pleasing form and one well suited to those limited uses which we must needs make of your space/time motivating requirements.

QUESTIONER: Was there a principle of motivation contained within the three hemispheres on the bottom, or were they just aesthetic, or were they landing gear?

RA: I am Ra. These were aesthetic and part of a system of propulsion. These hemispheres were not landing gear.

QUESTIONER: I am sorry to ask such stupid questions, but I am trying to determine something about space/time, time/space, and this very difficult area of the mechanism of evolution. I think it is central to the understanding of our evolution. However, I am not sure of this, and I may be wasting my time. Could Ra comment on whether I am wasting my time in this particular investigation or whether it would be fruitful?

RA: I am Ra. Since the concepts of space/time, or physics, and time/ space, or metaphysics, are mechanical, they are not central to the spiritual evolution of the mind/body/spirit complex. The study of love and light is far more productive in its motion towards unity in those entities pondering such concepts. However, this material is, shall we say, of some small interest and is harmless.

QUESTIONER: I was asking these questions primarily to understand or to build a base for an attempt to get a little bit of enlightenment on the way that time/space and space/time are related to the evolution of the mind/body/spirit complex, so that I could better understand the techniques of evolution. For instance, you stated, "the potential difference may be released and polarity changed after an entity has learned/taught the lessons of love of self" if the entity is a positive entity that has found itself in negative time/space and has had to incarnate into negative space/time. What I was trying to do was build a base for an attempt to get a slight understanding of what you meant by this statement that potential difference may be released and polar- ity changed after the above step. I am very interested in knowing, if placed in a negative time/space, why it is necessary to incarnate in negative space/time and learn/teach love of self and develop—I guess—a sixth-density level of polarity before you can release that potential difference. Could you speak on that subject?

RA: I am Ra. This will be the last full query of this working.
    The entity which incarnates into negative space/time will not find it possible to maintain any significant positive polarity, as negativity, when pure, is a type of gravity well, shall we say, pulling all into it. Thus the entity, while remembering its learned and preferred polarity, must needs make use of the catalyst given and recapitulate the lessons of service to self in order to build up enough polarity in order to cause the potential to occur for reversal.
    There is much in this line of questioning which is somewhat mud- dled. May we, at this point, allow the questioner to rephrase the question or to turn the direction of query more towards that which is the heart of its concern.

QUESTIONER: I will, at the next session, then attempt to turn more toward the heart. I was attempting in this session to get at a point that I thought was central to the evolution of spirit, but I seem to have gone awry. It is sometimes very, very difficult for me to question wisely in these areas.

I will just ask if there is anything that we can do to enhance the contact or to make the instrument more comfortable?

RA: I am Ra. You are most conscientious, and the alignments are especially good. We thank you, my friends, and have been glad to speak with you. We are attempting to be of the greatest aid to you by taking care not to deplete this instrument. Thus, although a reserve remains, we will attempt from this working onward to keep this reserve, for this instrument has arranged its subconscious to accept this configuration.

I am Ra. You are all doing well, my friends. We leave you in the love and in the light of the One Infinite Creator. Go forth, therefore, rejoicing and glorying in the power and in the peace of the One Infinite Creator. Adonai.

Session 71,
September 18, 1981

RA: I am Ra. I greet you in the love and in the light of the One Infinite Creator. We communicate now.

QUESTIONER: Could you first please give me the condition of the instrument?

RA: I am Ra. It is as previously stated, with the exception of a slight improvement in the vital energy distortions. One may note to the support group, without infringement, that it is well to aid the instrument in the reminders that while physical complex distortions remain as they are, it is not advisable to use the increased vital energies for physical complex activities as this will take a somewhat harsh toll.

QUESTIONER: In this session I hope to ask several different questions to establish a point of entry into an investigation that will be fruitful. I would first ask if it is possible to increase polarity without increasing harvestability?

RA: I am Ra. The connection between polarization and harvestability is most important in third-density harvest. In this density an increase in the serving of others or the serving of self will almost inevitably increase the ability of an entity to enjoy a higher intensity of light.

Thus in this density, we may say, it is hardly possible to polarize without increasing in harvestability.

QUESTIONER: This would probably be possible in the higher densities, such as the fifth density. Is this correct?

RA: I am Ra. In fifth-density harvest, polarization has very little to do with harvestability.

QUESTIONER: Would you explain the concept of working with the unmanifested being in third density to accelerate evolution?

RA: I am Ra. This is a many-layered question, and which stria we wish to expose is questionable. Please restate, giving any further depth of information requested, if possible.

QUESTIONER: Define, please, the unmanifested being.

RA: I am Ra. We may see that you wish to pursue the deeper strata of information. We shall, therefore, answer in a certain way which does not exhaust the query but is designed to move beneath the outer teachings somewhat.

The unmanifested being is, as we have said, that being which exists and does its work without reference to or aid from other-selves. To move into this concept, you may see the inevitable connection between the unmanifested self and the metaphysical or time/space analog of the space/time self. The activities of meditation, contemplation, and what may be called the internal balancing of thoughts and reactions are those activities of the unmanifested self more closely aligned with the metaphysical self.

QUESTIONER: As an entity goes through the death process in third density, it finds itself in time/space. It finds itself in a different set of circumstances. Would you please describe the circumstances or properties of time/space and then the process of healing of incarnative experiences that some entities encounter?

RA: I am Ra. Although this query is difficult to answer adequately, due to the limitations of your space/time sound vibration complexes, we shall respond to the best of our ability.

The hallmark of time/space is the inequity between time and space. In your space/time the spatial orientation of material causes a tangible framework for illusion. In time/space the inequity is upon the shoulders of that property known to you as time. This property renders entities and experiences intangible in a relative sense. In your framework, each particle or core vibration moves at a velocity which approaches what you call the speed of light from the direction of supraluminal velocities.

Thus the time/space or metaphysical experience is that which is very finely tuned and, although an analog of space/time, lacking in its tangible characteristics. In these metaphysical planes there is a great deal of what you call time which is used to review and re-review the biases and learn/teachings of a prior, as you would call it, space/time incarnation.

The extreme fluidity of these regions makes it possible for much to be penetrated which must needs be absorbed before the process of healing of an entity may be accomplished. Each entity is located in a somewhat immobile state, much as you are located in space/time in a somewhat immobile state in time. In this immobile space the entity has been placed by the form maker and Higher Self so that it may be in the proper configuration for learn/teaching that which it has received in the space/time incarnation.

Depending upon this time/space locus, there will be certain helpers which assist in this healing process. The process involves seeing in full the experience, seeing it against the backdrop of the mind/body/spirit complex total experience, forgiving the self for all missteps as regards the missed guideposts during the incarnation, and, finally, the careful assessment of the next necessities for learning. This is done entirely by the Higher Self until an entity has become conscious in space/time of the process and means of spiritual evolution, at which time the entity will consciously take part in all decisions.

QUESTIONER: Is the process in positive time/space identical with the process in negative time/space for this healing?

RA: I am Ra. The process in space/time of the forgiveness and acceptance is much like that in time/space, in that the qualities of the process are analogous. However, while in space/time it is not possible to determine the course of events beyond the incarnation, but only to correct present imbalances. In time/space, upon the other hand, it is not possible to correct any unbalanced actions but rather to perceive the imbalances and thusly forgive the self for that which is.

The decisions then are made to set up the possibility/probabilities of correcting these imbalances in what you call future space/time experiences. The advantage of time/space is that of the fluidity of the grand overview. The advantage of space/time is that, working in darkness with a tiny candle, one may correct imbalances.

QUESTIONER: If an entity has chosen the negative polarization, are the processes of healing and review similar for the negative path?

RA: I am Ra. This is correct.

QUESTIONER: Are the processes that we are talking about processes that occur on many planets in our Milky Way Galaxy, or do they occur on all planets, or what percentage?

RA: I am Ra. These processes occur upon all planets which have given birth to sub-Logoi such as yourselves. The percentage of inhabited planets is approximately 10 percent.

QUESTIONER: What percentage of stars, roughly, have planetary systems?

RA: I am Ra. This is unimportant information, but harmless. Approximately 32 percent of stars have planets as you know them, while another 6 percent have some sort of clustering material which upon some densities might be inhabitable.

QUESTIONER: This would tell me that roughly 3 percent of all stars have inhabited planets. This process of evolution is in effect throughout the known universe then. Is this correct?

RA: I am Ra. This octave of infinite knowledge of the One Creator is as it is throughout the One Infinite Creation, with variations programmed by sub-Logoi of what you call major galaxies and minor galaxies. These variations are not significant but may be compared to various regions of geographical location sporting various ways of pronouncing the same sound vibration complex or concept.

QUESTIONER: It seems to me from this that the sub-Logos such as our sun uses free will to modify only slightly a much more general idea of created evolution, so that the general plan of created evolution then seems to be uniform throughout the One Infinite Creation. The process is for the sub-Logoi to grow through the densities and, under the first distortion, find their way back to the original thought. Is this correct?

RA: I am Ra. This is correct.

QUESTIONER: Then each entity is of a path that leads to one destination.

This is like many, many roads that travel through many, many places but eventually merge into one large center. Is this correct?

RA: I am Ra. This is correct but somewhat wanting in depth of description. More applicable would be the thought that each entity contains within it all of the densities and sub-densities of the octave, so that in each entity, no matter whither its choices lead it, its great internal blueprint is one with all others. Thusly its experiences will fall into the patterns of the journey back to the original Logos. This is done through free will, but the materials from which choices can be made are one blueprint.

QUESTIONER: You have made the statement that pure negativity acts as a gravity well, pulling all into it. I was wondering first if pure positivity has precisely the same effect? Could you answer that, please?

RA: I am Ra. This is incorrect. Positivity has a much weaker effect due to the strong element of recognition of free will in any positivity approaching purity. Thus, although the negatively oriented entity may find it difficult to polarize negatively in the midst of such resounding harmony, it will not find it impossible.

Upon the other hand, the negative polarization is one which does not accept the concept of the free will of other-selves. Thusly, in a social complex whose negativity approaches purity, the pull upon other-selves is constant. A positively oriented entity in such a situation would desire for other-selves to have their free will and thusly would find itself removed from its ability to exercise its own free will, for the free will of negatively oriented entities is bent upon conquest.

QUESTIONER: Could you please comment on the accuracy of these statements. I am going to talk in general about the concept of magic and first define it as the ability to create changes in consciousness at will. Is this an acceptable definition?

RA: I am Ra. This definition is acceptable in that it places upon the adept the burden it shall bear. It may be better understood by referring back to an earlier query, in your measurement, within this working having to do with the unmanifested self. In magic, one is working with one's unmanifested self in body, in mind, and in spirit, the mixture depending upon the nature of the working.

These workings are facilitated by the enhancement of the activation of the indigo-ray energy center. The indigo-ray energy center is fed, as are all energy centers, by experience, but far more than the others is fed by what we have called the disciplines of the personality.

QUESTIONER: I will state that the objective of the white magical ritual is to create a change in consciousness of a group. Is this correct?

RA: I am Ra. Not necessarily. It is possible for what you term white magic to be worked for the purpose of altering only the self or the place of working. This is done in the knowledge that to aid the self in polarization towards love and light is to aid the planetary vibration.

QUESTIONER: The change in consciousness should result in a greater distortion towards service to others, towards unity with all, and towards knowing in order to serve. Is this correct, and are there any other desired results?

RA: I am Ra. These are commendable phrases. The heart of white magic is the experience of the joy of union with the Creator. This joy will of necessity radiate throughout the life experience of the positive adept. It is for this reason that sexual magic is not restricted solely to the negatively oriented polarizing adepts but, when most carefully used, has its place in high magic as it, when correctly pursued, joins body, mind, and spirit with the One Infinite Creator.

Any purpose which you may frame should, we suggest, take into consideration this basic union with the One Infinite Creator, for this union will result in service to others of necessity.

QUESTIONER: There are, shall I say, certain rules of white magic. I will read these few, and I would like you to comment on the philosophical content or basis of these and add to this list any of importance that I have neglected. First, a special place of working preferably constructed by the practitioners; second, a special signal or key such as a ring to summon the magical personality; third, special clothing worn only for the workings; fourth, a specific time of day; fifth, a series of ritual sound vibratory complexes designed to create the desired mental distortion; sixth, a group objective for each session. Could you comment on this list, please?

RA: I am Ra. To comment upon this list is to play the mechanic which views the instruments of the orchestra and adjusts and tunes the instruments. You will note these are mechanical details. The art does not lie herein.

The one item of least import is what you call the time of day. This is important in those experiential nexi wherein the entities search for the metaphysical experience without conscious control over the search. The repetition of workings gives this search structure. In this particular group the structure is available without the need for inevitable sameness of times of working. We may note that this regularity is always helpful.

QUESTIONER: You stated in a previous session that Ra searched for some time to find a group such as this one. I would assume that this search was for the purpose of communicating the Law of One. Is this correct?

RA: I am Ra. This is partially correct. We also, as we have said, wished to attempt to make reparation for distortions of this law set in motion by our naive actions of your past.

QUESTIONER: Can you tell me if we have covered the necessary material at this point to, if published, make the necessary reparations for the naive actions?

RA: I am Ra. We mean no disrespect for your service, but we do not expect to make full reparations for these distortions. We may, however, offer our thoughts in the attempt. The attempt is far more important to us than the completeness of the result. The nature of your language is such that what is distorted cannot, to our knowledge, be fully undistorted but only illuminated somewhat. In response to your desire to see the relationship betwixt space/time and time/space, may we say that we conducted this search in time/space, for in this illusion one may quite readily see entities as vibratory complexes and groups as harmonics within vibratory complexes.

QUESTIONER: I see the most important aspect of this communication as being a vehicle of partial enlightenment for those incarnate now who have become aware of their part in their own evolutionary process. Am I correct in this assumption?

RA: I am Ra. You are correct. We may note that this is the goal of all artifacts and experiences which entities may come into contact with, and is not only the property of Ra or this contact.

We find that this instrument has neglected to continue to remind its self of the need for holding some portion of energy back for reserve. This is recommended as a portion of the inner program to be reinstated, as it will lengthen the number of workings we may have. This is acceptable to us. The transferred energy grows quite, quite low. We must leave you shortly. Is there a brief query at this time?

QUESTIONER: Is there anything that we can do to improve the contact or to make the instrument more comfortable?

RA: I am Ra. You are conscientious. Remain most fastidious about the alignments of the appurtenances. We thank you. I am Ra. I leave you in the love and in the glorious light of the Infinite Creator. Go forth, therefore, rejoicing in the power and in the peace of the One Infinite Creator. Adonai.

Session 72,
October 14, 1981

RA: I am Ra. I greet you in the love and in the light of the One Infinite Creator. We communicate now.

QUESTIONER: Could you first give me an indication of the instrument's condition?

RA: I am Ra. This instrument's physical energy distortions are as previously stated. The vital energy level has become distorted from normal levels, somewhat downward, due to the distortion in this instrument's mind complex activity that it has been responsible for the, shall we say, difficulties in achieving the appropriate configuration for this contact.

QUESTIONER: Was the banishing ritual that we performed of any effect in purifying the place of working and the screening of influences that we do not wish?

RA: I am Ra. This is quite correct.

QUESTIONER: Can you tell me what I can do to improve the effectiveness of the ritual?

RA: I am Ra. No.

QUESTIONER: Can you tell me what caused the instrument to become in a condition toward unconsciousness in the last two meditations prior to this one, to such an extent that we discontinued them?

RA: I am Ra. We can.

QUESTIONER: Would you please tell me then?

RA: I am Ra. The entity which greets this instrument from the Orion group first attempted to cause the mind/body/spirit complex, which you may call spirit, to leave the physical complex of yellow ray in the deluded belief that it was preparing for the Ra contact. You are familiar with this tactic and its consequences. The instrument, with no pause, upon feeling this greeting, called for the grounding within the physical complex by requesting that the hand be held. Thus the greatest aim of the Orion entity was not achieved. However, it discovered that those present were not capable of distinguishing between unconsciousness with the mind/body/spirit intact and the trance state in which the mind/body/spirit complex is not present.

Therefore, it applied to the fullest extent the greeting which causes the dizziness and in meditation without protection caused, in this instrument, simple unconsciousness, as in what you would call fainting or vertigo. The Orion entity consequently used this tactic to stop the Ra contact from having the opportunity to be accomplished.

QUESTIONER: The instrument has scheduled an operation on her hand next month. If the general anesthetic is used to produce the unconscious state, will this or any other parameters of the operation allow for any inroads by the Orion entities?

RA: I am Ra. It is extremely improbable due to the necessity for the intention of the mind/body/spirit complex, when departing the yellow-ray physical complex, to be serving the Creator in the most specific fashion. The attitude of one approaching such an experience as you describe would not be approaching the unconscious state with such an attitude.

QUESTIONER: We have here, I believe, a very important principle with respect to the Law of One. You have stated that the attitude of the individual is of paramount importance for the Orion entity to be able to be effective. Would you please explain how this mechanism works with respect to the Law of One, and why the attitude of the entity is of paramount importance and why this allows for action by the Orion entity?

RA: I am Ra. The Law of Confusion or Free Will is utterly paramount in the workings of the infinite creation. That which is intended has as much intensity of attraction to the polar opposite as the intensity of the intention or desire.

Thus, those whose desires are shallow or transitory experience only ephemeral configurations of what might be called the magical circumstance. There is a turning point, a fulcrum which swings as a mind/body/spirit complex tunes its will to service. If this will and desire is for service to others, the corresponding polarity will be activated. In the circumstance of this group, there are three such wills acting as one with the instrument in the, shall we say, central position of fidelity to service. This is as it must be for the balance of the working and the continuance of the contact. Our vibratory complex is one-pointed in these workings also, and our will to serve is also of some degree of purity. This has created the attraction of the polar opposite which you experience.

We may note that such a configuration of free will, one-pointed in service to others, also has the potential for the alerting of a great mass of light strength. This positive light strength, however, operates also under free will and must be invoked. We could not speak to this and shall not guide you, for the nature of this contact is such that the purity of your free will must, above all things, be preserved. Thus you wend your way through experiences, discovering those biases which may be helpful.

QUESTIONER: The negatively oriented entities who contact us and others on this planet are limited by the first distortion. They have obviously been limited by the banishing ritual just performed. Could you describe, with respect to free will, how they limit themselves in order to work within the first distortion and how the banishing ritual itself works?

RA: I am Ra. This query has several portions. Firstly, those of negative polarity do not operate with respect to free will unless it is necessary. They call themselves and will infringe whenever they feel it possible.

Secondly, they are limited by the great Law of Confusion in that, for the most part, they are unable to enter this planetary sphere of influence and are able to use the windows of time/space distortion only insofar as there is some calling to balance the positive calling. Once they are here, their desire is conquest.

Thirdly, in the instance of this instrument's being removed permanently from this space/time, it is necessary to allow the instrument to leave its yellow-ray physical complex of its free will. Thus trickery has been attempted.

The use of the light forms being generated is such as to cause such entities to discover a wall through which they cannot pass. This is due to the energy complexes of the light beings and aspects of the One Infinite Creator invoked and evoked in the building of the wall of light.

QUESTIONER: Everything that we experience with respect to this contact, our distortion toward knowledge in order to serve, the Orion entity's distortion towards reducing the effectiveness of this contact, all of this is a result of the first distortion, as I see it, in creating the totally free atmosphere for the Creator to become more knowledgeable of Itself through the interplay of its portions, one with respect to the other. Is my view correct with respect to what I have just said?

RA: I am Ra. Yes.

QUESTIONER: In the last session you mentioned that if the instrument used any of the increased vital energy that she experiences for physical activity that she would pay a "harsh toll." Could you tell me the nature of that harsh toll and why it would be experienced?

RA: I am Ra. The physical energy level is a measure of the amount of available energy of the body complex of a mind/body/spirit complex. The vital energy measurement is one which expresses the amount of energy of being of the mind/body/spirit complex.

This entity has great distortions in the direction of mind complex activity, spirit complex activity, and that great conduit to the Creator, the will. Therefore, this instrument's vital energy, even in the absence of any physical reserve measurable, is quite substantial. However, the use of this energy of will, mind, and spirit for the things of the physical complex causes a far greater distortion in the lessening of the vital energy than would the use of this energy for those things which are in the deepest desires and will of the mind/body/spirit complex. In this entity these desires are for service to the Creator. This entity sees all service as service to the Creator, and this is why we have cautioned the support group and the instrument itself in this regard. All services are not equal in depth of distortion. The overuse of this vital energy is, to be literal, the rapid removal of life force.

QUESTIONER: You mentioned that the large amount of light that is available. Could this group, by proper ritual, use this for recharging the vital energy of the instrument?

RA: I am Ra. This is correct. However, we caution against any working which raises up any personality; rather it is well to be fastidious in your working.

QUESTIONER: Could you explain what you mean by "raises up any personality"?

RA: I am Ra. Clues, we may offer. Explanation is infringement. We can only ask that you realize that all are One.

QUESTIONER: We have included "Shin" in the banishing ritual, "Yod-Heh-Vau-Heh" to make it "Yod-Heh-Shin-Vau-Heh." Is this helpful?

RA: I am Ra. This is helpful especially to the instrument whose distortions vibrate greatly in congruency with this sound vibration complex.

QUESTIONER: We will in the future have group meditations. I am concerned about protection for the instrument if she is once more a channel in these meditations. Is there an optimum time or limiting amount of time for the banishing ritual to be effective, or if we continued daily to purify the place of working with the banishing ritual, would this carry over for long periods of time, or must the ritual be done immediately prior to the meditations?

RA: I am Ra. Your former assumption is more nearly correct.

QUESTIONER: Is there any danger now, with the precautions that we are taking, of the instrument being led away by the Orion entity?

RA: I am Ra. The opportunities for the Orion entity are completely dependent upon the instrument's condition of awareness and readiness. We would suggest that this instrument is still too much the neophyte to open its self to questions since that is the format used by Ra. As the instrument grows in awareness this precaution may become unnecessary.

QUESTIONER: Why is there no protection at the floor or bottom of the banishing ritual, and should there be?

RA: I am Ra. This will be the last full query of this working.
The development of the psychic greeting is possible only through the energy centers, starting from a station which you might call within the violet ray moving through the adept's energy center and therefrom

towards the target of opportunity. Depending upon the vibratory nature and purpose of greeting, be it positive or negative, the entity will be energized or blocked in the desired way.

We of Ra approach this instrument in narrow-band contact through violet ray. Others might pierce down through this ray to any energy center. We, for instance, make great use of this instrument's blue-ray energy center as we are attempting to communicate our distortion/understandings of the Law of One.

The entity of Orion pierces the same violet ray and moves to two places to attempt most of its nonphysical opportunities. It activates the green-ray energy center while further blocking indigo-ray energy center. This combination causes confusion in the instrument and subsequent over-activity in unwise proportions in physical complex workings. It simply seeks out the distortions pre-incarnatively programmed and developed in incarnative state.

The energies of life itself, being the One Infinite Creator, flow from the south pole of the body seen in its magnetic form. Thus only the Creator may, through the feet, enter the energy shell of the body to any effect. The effects of the adept are those from the upper direction, and thus the building of the wall of light is quite propitious.

May we ask if there are any shorter queries at this time?

QUESTIONER: I would just ask if there is anything that we could do to make the instrument more comfortable or to improve the contact?

RA: I am Ra. This instrument has some increased distortion in the region of the neck. Some attention here might provide greater comfort. All is well, my friends. The forbearance and patience observed by Ra are commendable. Continue in this fastidiousness of purpose and care for the appropriate configurations for contact, and our continuance of contact will continue to be possible. This is acceptable to us.

I am Ra. I leave you, my friends, glorying in the love and the light of the One Infinite Creator. Go forth, then, rejoicing in the power and in the peace of the One Infinite Creator. Adonai.

Session 73,
October 21, 1981

RA: I am Ra. I greet you in the love and in the light of the One Infinite Creator. We communicate now.

QUESTIONER: Could you please give me an indication of the instrument's condition?

RA: I am Ra. It is as previously stated, with the exception of the vital energy level which is distorted more nearly towards that which is normal for this entity.

QUESTIONER: Has the banishing ritual that we have performed been helpful for this contact?

RA: I am Ra. The ritual described has gained with each working in making efficacious the purity of contact needed not only for the Ra contact but for any working of the adept.

QUESTIONER: Thank you. I would like to thank Ra at this time for the opportunity to be of service to those on this sphere who would want to have the information that we gain here.

You stated that free will, one-pointed in service to others, had the potential of alerting a great mass of light strength. I assume that the same holds precisely true for the service-to-self polarity. Is this correct?

RA: I am Ra. This is incorrect but subtly so. In invocation and evocation of what may be termed negative entities or qualities, the expression alerts the positively oriented equivalent. However, those upon the service-to-others path wait to be called and can only send love.

QUESTIONER: What I was trying to get at was that this alerting of light strength is, as I see it, a process that must be totally a function of free will, as you say, and as the desire and will and purity of desire of the adept increases, the alerting of light strength increases. Is this part of it the same for both the positive and negative potentials, and am I correct with this statement?

RA: I am Ra. To avoid confusion we shall simply restate for clarity your correct assumption.

Those who are upon the service-to-others path may call upon the light strength in direct proportion to the strength and purity of their will to serve. Those upon the service-to-self path may call upon the dark strength in direct proportion to the strength and purity of their will to serve.

QUESTIONER: I will undoubtedly make many errors in my statements today because what I am trying to do is guess at how this works, and let you correct me. In considering the exercise of the Middle Pillar, I have thought it might be wrong in that in it the adept sees or visualizes the light moving downward from the crown chakra down to the feet. Ra has stated that the Creator enters from the feet and moves upward, that this spiraling light enters from the feet and moves upward. It seems to me that the adept alerting the light strength, in visualizing the use of this, would visualize it entering the feet and energizing, first, the red energy center and then moving upward through the energy centers in that fashion. Is this correct?

RA: I am Ra. No.

QUESTIONER: Could you tell me where I am wrong in that statement?

RA: I am Ra. Yes.

QUESTIONER: Would you please do that?

RA: I am Ra. There are two concepts with which you deal. The first is the great way of the development of the light in the microcosmic mind/body/spirit. It is assumed that an adept will have its energy centers functioning smoothly and in a balanced manner to its best effort before a magical working. All magical workings are based upon evocation and/or invocation.

The first invocation of any magical working is that invocation of the magical personality as you are familiar with this term. In the working of which you speak, the first station is the beginning of the invocation of this magical personality, which is invoked by the motion of putting on something. Since you do not have an item of apparel or talisman, the gesture which you have made is appropriate.

The second station is the evocation of the great cross of life. This is an extension of the magical personality to become the Creator. Again, all invocations and evocations are drawn through the violet energy center. This may then be continued towards whatever energy centers are desired to be used.

QUESTIONER: Then will you speak of the difference between the spiraling light that enters through the feet and the light invoked through the crown chakra?

RA: I am Ra. The action of the upward-spiraling light drawn by the will to meet the inner light of the One Infinite Creator may be likened to the beating of the heart and the movement of the muscles surrounding the lungs and all the other functions of the parasympathetic nervous system. The calling of the adept may be likened to those nerve and muscle actions over which the mind/body/spirit complex has conscious control.

QUESTIONER: Previously you stated that where the two directions meet, you have a measure of the development of the particular mind/body/spirit complex. Am I correct?

RA: I am Ra. This is correct.

QUESTIONER: It would seem to me that the visualization of the invocation would be dependent upon what the use was to be of the light. The use could be for healing, communication, or for the general awareness of the creation and the Creator. Would you please speak on this process and my correctness in making this assumption?

RA: I am Ra. We shall offer some thoughts, though it is doubtful that we may exhaust this subject. Each visualization, regardless of the point of the working, begins with some work within the indigo ray. As you may be aware, the ritual which you have begun is completely working within the indigo ray. This is well for it is the gateway. From this beginning, light may be invoked for communication or for healing.

You may note that in the ritual which we offered you to properly begin the Ra workings, the first focus is upon the Creator. We would further note a point which is both subtle and of some interest. The upward-spiraling light developed in its path by the will and, ultimately reaching a high place of mating with the inward fire of the One Creator, still is only preparation for the work upon the mind/body/spirit which may be done by the adept. There is some crystallization of the energy centers used during each working, so that the magician becomes more and more that which it seeks.

More importantly, the time/space mind/body/spirit analog, which is evoked as the magical personality, has its only opportunity to gain rapidly from the experience of the catalytic action available to the third-density space/time mind/body/spirit. Thus the adept is aiding the Creator greatly by offering great catalyst to a greater portion of the creation which is identified as the mind/body/spirit totality of an entity.

QUESTIONER: Desire and will are the factors in this process. Is this correct?

RA: I am Ra. We would add one quality. In the magical personality, desire, will, and polarity are the keys.

QUESTIONER: Many so-called evangelists which we have in our society at present have great desire and very great will, and possibly great polarity, but it seems to me that in many cases that there is a lack of awareness that creates a less-than-effective working in the magical sense. Am I correct in this analysis?

RA: I am Ra. You are partially correct. In examining the polarity of a service-to-others working, the free will must be seen as paramount. Those entities of which you speak are attempting to generate positive changes in consciousness while abridging free will. This causes the blockage of the magical nature of the working except in those cases wherein an entity freely desires to accept the working of the evangelist, as you have called it.

QUESTIONER: What was the orientation with respect to this type of communication for the one known as Jesus of Nazareth?

RA: I am Ra. You may have read some of this entity's workings. It offered itself as teacher to those mind/body/spirit complexes which gathered to hear and even then spoke as through a veil so as to leave room for those not wishing to hear. When this entity was asked to heal, it oft times did so, always ending the working with two admonitions: firstly, that the entity healed had been healed by its faith—that is, its ability to allow and accept changes through the violet ray into the gateway of intelligent energy; secondly, saying always, "Tell no one." These are the workings which attempt the maximal quality of free will while maintaining fidelity to the positive purity of the working.

QUESTIONER: An observation of the working itself by another entity would seem to me to partially abridge free will, in that a seemingly magical occurrence had taken place as the result of the working of an adept. This could be extended to any phenomenon which is other than normal or acceptable. Could you speak on this paradox that is immediately the problem of anyone doing healing?

RA: I am Ra. We are humble messengers of the Law of One. To us there are no paradoxes. The workings which seem magical and, therefore, seem to infringe upon free will do not, in themselves, do so, for the distortions of perception are as many as the witnesses, and each witness sees what it desires to see. Infringement upon free will occurs in this circumstance only if the entity doing the working ascribes the authorship of this event to its self or its own skills. He who states that no working comes from it but only through it is not infringing upon free will.

QUESTIONER: The one known as Jesus accumulated twelve disciples. What was his purpose in having these disciples with him?

RA: I am Ra. What is the purpose of teach/learning if there be no learn/teachers? Those drawn to this entity were accepted by this entity without regard for any outcome. This entity accepted the honor/duty placed upon it by its nature and its sense that to speak was its mission.

QUESTIONER: In the exercise of the fire, I assume the healer would be working with the same energy that we spoke of as entering through the crown chakra. Is this correct?

RA: I am Ra. This is correct, with some additional notation necessary for your thought in continuing this line of study. When the magical personality has been seated in the green-ray energy center for healing work, the energy then may be seen to be the crystalline center through which body energy is channeled. Thus this particular form of healing uses both the energy of the adept and the energy of the upward-spiraling light. As the green-ray center becomes more brilliant, and we would note this brilliance does not imply over-activation but rather crystallization, the energy of the green-ray center of the body complex spirals twice; firstly, clockwise from the green-ray energy center to the right shoulder, through the head, the right elbow, down through the solar plexus, and to the left hand. This sweeps all the body complex energy into a channel which then rotates the great circle clockwise again from right—we correct this instrument—from the left to the feet, to the right hand, to the crown, to the left hand, and so forth.

Thus the incoming body energy, crystallized, regularized, and channeled by the adept's personality reaching to the green-ray energy center, may then pour out the combined energies of the adept which is incarnate, thus offering the service of healing to an entity requesting that service. This basic situation is accomplished as well when there is an entity which is working through a channel to heal.

QUESTIONER: Can you tell me how this transfer of light, I believe it would be, would affect the patient to be healed?

RA: I am Ra. The effect is that of polarization. The entity may or may not accept any percentage of this polarized life energy which is being offered. In the occasion of the laying on of hands, this energy is more specifically channeled and the opportunity for acceptance of this energy similarly more specific.

It may be seen that the King's Chamber effect is not attempted in this form of working but rather the addition to one, whose energies are low, of the opportunity for the building up of those energies. Many of your distortions called illnesses may be aided by such means.

QUESTIONER: As a general statement, which you can correct, the overall picture, as I see it, of the healer and patient is that the one to be healed has, because of a blockage in one of the energy centers or more—we will just consider one particular problem—because of this energy center blockage, the upward-spiraling light which creates one of the seven bodies has been blocked from the maintenance of that body, and this has resulted in the distortion from the perfection of that body which we call disease or a bodily anomaly which is other than perfect. The healer, having suitably configured its energy centers, is able to channel light, the downward-pouring light, though its properly configured energy centers to the one to be healed. If the one to be healed has the mental configuration of acceptance of this light, the light then enters the physical complex and reconfigures the distortion that is created by the original blockage. I am sure that I have made some mistakes in all this. Would you please correct them?

RA: I am Ra. Your mistakes were small. We would not, at this time, attempt a great deal of refinement of that statement, as there is preliminary material which will undoubtedly come forward. We may say that there are various forms of healing. In many, only the energy of the adept is used. In the exercise of fire, some physical complex energy is also channeled.

We might note further that when the one wishing to be healed, though sincere, remains unhealed, as you call this distortion, you may consider pre-incarnative choices and your more helpful aid to such an entity may be the suggestion that it meditate upon the affirmative uses of whatever limitations it might experience. We would also note that in these cases, the indigo-ray workings are often of aid.

Other than these notes, we do not wish to further comment upon your statement at this working.

QUESTIONER: It seems to me that the primary thing of importance for those on the service-to-others path is the development of an attitude which I can only describe as a vibration. This attitude would be developed through meditation, ritual, and the developing appreciation for the creation or Creator, which results in a state of mind that can only be expressed by me as an increase in vibration or oneness with all. Could you expand and correct that statement?

RA: I am Ra. We shall not correct this statement but shall expand upon it by suggesting that to those qualities, you may add the living day by day and moment by moment, for the true adept lives more and more as it is.

QUESTIONER: Thank you. Could you tell me of the number of possible energy transfers between two or more mind/body/spirit complexes. Is it very large, or are there few?

RA: I am Ra. The number is infinite, for is not each mind/body/spirit complex unique?

QUESTIONER: Could you define this statement: "energy transfer between two mind/body/spirit complexes"?

RA: I am Ra. This will be the last full query of this working. This entity still has transferred energy available, but we find rapidly increasing distortions towards pain in the neck, the dorsal area, and the wrists and manual appendages.

The physical energy transfer may be done numerous ways. We shall give two examples. Each begins with some sense of the self as Creator or in some way the magical personality being invoked. This may be consciously or unconsciously done. Firstly, that exercise of which we have spoken called the exercise of fire: this is, through physical energy transfer, not that which is deeply involved in the body complex combinations. Thusly the transfer is subtle, and each transfer unique in what is offered and what is accepted. At this point we may note that this is the cause for the infinite array of possible energy transfers.

The second energy transfer of which we would speak is the sexual energy transfer. This takes place upon a nonmagical level by all those entities which vibrate green ray active. It is possible, as in the case of this instrument which dedicates itself to the service of the One Infinite Creator, to further refine this energy transfer. When the other-self also dedicates itself in service to the One Infinite Creator, the transfer is doubled. Then the amount of energy transferred is dependent only upon the amount of polarized sexual energy created and released. There are refinements from this point onward, leading to the realm of the high sexual magic.

In the realm of the mental bodies, there are variations of mental energy transferred. This is, again, dependent upon the knowledge sought and the knowledge offered. The most common mental energy transfer is that of the teacher and the pupil. The amount of energy is dependent upon the quality of this offering upon the part of the teacher and regards the purity of the desire to serve, and the quality of information offered and, upon the part of the student, the purity of the desire to learn and the quality of the mind vibratory complex which receives knowledge.

Another form of mental energy transfer is that of the listener and the speaker. When the speaker is experiencing mental/emotional complex distortions towards anguish, sorrow, or other mental pain, from what we have said before, you may perhaps garner knowledge of the variations possible in this transfer.

The spiritual energy transfers are at the heart of all energy transfers as a knowledge of self and other-self as Creator is paramount, and this is spiritual work. The varieties of spiritual energy transfer include those things of which we have spoken this day as we spoke upon the subject of the adept.

Are there any brief queries before we leave this working?

QUESTIONER: Only if there is anything we can do to improve the comfort of the instrument and the contact, and secondly, is there anything that you wish not published in today's session?

RA: I am Ra. We call your attention to two items. Firstly, it is well that the candle which spirals 10° each working be never allowed to gutter, as this would cause imbalance in the alignment of the appurtenances in their protective role for this instrument. Secondly, we might suggest attention to the neck area so that the cushion upon which it is supported be more comfortable. This difficulty has abbreviated many workings.

We thank you, my friends, for your conscientiousness and your fastidiousness with regard to these appurtenances, which, as our workings proceed, seems to be increasing. Secondly, your decisions are completely your own as to that material which you may wish published from this working.

I am Ra. I leave you glorying in the love and in the light of the One Infinite Creator. Go forth, then, rejoicing in the power and in the peace of the One Infinite Creator. Adonai.

Session 74,
October 28, 1981

RA: I am Ra. I greet you in the love and in the light of the One Infinite Creator. We communicate now.

QUESTIONER: Would you first please give me the condition of the instrument?

RA: I am Ra. It is as previously stated.

QUESTIONER: Before we get to new material, in the last session there seems to be a small error that I corrected then having to do with this statement: "no working comes from it but only through it." Was this an error in the transmission? What caused this?

RA: I am Ra. This instrument, while fully open to our narrow-band contact, at times experiences a sudden strengthening of the distortion which you call pain. This weakens the contact momentarily. This type of increased distortion has been occurring in this instrument's bodily complex with more frequency in the time period which you may term the previous fortnight. Although it is not normally a phenomenon which causes difficulties in transmission, it did so twice in the previous working. Both times it was necessary to correct or rectify the contact.

QUESTIONER: Could you please describe the trance state? I am somewhat confused as to how, in a trance, pain can affect the instrument, since I was of the opinion that there would be no feeling of pain by the bodily complex in the trance state?

RA: I am Ra. This is correct. The instrument has no awareness of this or other sensations. However, we of Ra use the yellow-ray-activated physical complex as a channel through which to speak. As the mind/body/spirit complex of the instrument leaves this physical shell in our keeping, it is finely adjusted to our contact.

However, the distortion which you call pain, when sufficiently severe, mitigates against proper contact and, when the increased distortion is violent, can cause the tuning of the channel to waver. This tuning must then be corrected, which we may do as the instrument offers us this opportunity freely.

QUESTIONER: In a previous session there was a question on the archetypical mind that was not fully answered. I would like to continue with the answer to that question. Could you please continue with that, or will it be necessary for me to read the entire question over again?

RA: I am Ra. As a general practice it is well to vibrate the query at the same space/time as the answer is desired. However, in this case it is acceptable to us that a note be inserted at this point in your recording of these sound vibratory complexes referring to the location of the query in previous workings.

[Note: This question was the last question asked in Session 67.]

The query, though thoughtful, is in some degree falling short of the realization of the nature of the archetypical mind. We may not teach/learn for any other to the extent that we become learn/teachers. Therefore, we shall make some general notations upon this interesting subject and allow the questioner to consider and further refine any queries.

The archetypical mind may be defined as that mind which is peculiar to the Logos of this planetary sphere. Thusly, unlike the great cosmic all-mind, it contains the material which it pleased the Logos to offer as refinements to the great cosmic beingness. The archetypical mind, then, is that which contains all facets which may affect mind or experience.

The Magician was named as a significant archetype. However, it was not recognized that this portion of the archetypical mind represents not a portion of the deep subconscious but the conscious mind and more especially the will. The archetype called by some the High Priestess, then, is the corresponding intuitive or subconscious faculty.

Let us observe the entity as it is in relationship to the archetypical mind. You may consider the possibilities of utilizing the correspondences between the mind/body/spirit in microcosm and the archetypical mind/body/spirit closely approaching the Creator. For instance, in your ritual performed to purify this place, you use the term "Ve Geburah." It is a correct assumption that this is a portion or aspect of the One Infinite Creator. However, there are various correspondences with the archetypical mind which may be more and more refined by the adept. "Ve Geburah" is the correspondence of Michael, of Mars, of the positive, of maleness. "Ve Gedulah" has correspondences to Jupiter, to femaleness, to the negative, to that portion of the Tree of Life concerned with Auriel.

We could go forward with more and more refinements of these two entries into the archetypical mind. We could discuss color correspondences, relationships with other archetypes, and so forth. This is the work of the adept, not the teach/learner. We may only suggest that there are systems of study which may address themselves to the aspects of the archetypical mind, and it is well to choose one and study carefully. It is more nearly well if the adept go beyond whatever has been written and make such correspondences that the archetype can be called upon at will.

QUESTIONER: I have a statement here that I am going to make and let you correct. I see that the disciplines of the personality feed the indigo-ray energy center and affect the power of the white magician by unblocking the lower energy centers, allowing for the free flow of the upward-spiraling light to reach the indigo center. Is this correct?

RA: I am Ra. No.

QUESTIONER: Will you please correct me?

RA: I am Ra. The indigo center is indeed most important for the work of the adept. However, it cannot, no matter how crystallized, correct to any extent whatsoever imbalances or blockages in other energy centers. They must needs be cleared seriatim from red upwards.

QUESTIONER: I'm not sure exactly if I understand this. The question is how do disciplines of the personality feed the indigo-ray energy center and affect the power of the white magician? Does that question make sense?

RA: I am Ra. Yes.

QUESTIONER: Would you answer it please?

RA: I am Ra. We would be happy to answer this query. We understood the previous query as being of other import. The indigo ray is the ray of the adept. There is an identification between the crystallization of that energy center and the improvement of the working of the mind/body/spirit as it begins to transcend space/time balancing and to enter the combined realms of space/time and time/space.

QUESTIONER: Let me see if I have a wrong opinion here of the effect of disciplines of the personality. I was assuming that the discipline of the personality to, shall we say, have a balanced attitude toward a single fellow entity would properly clear and balance, to some extent, the orange-ray energy center. Is this correct?

RA: I am Ra. We cannot say that you speak incorrectly, but merely less than completely. The disciplined personality, when faced with an other-self, has all centers balanced according to its unique balance. Thusly the other-self looks in a mirror seeing its self.

QUESTIONER: The disciplines of the personality are the paramount work of any who have become consciously aware of the process of evolution. Am I correct on that statement?

RA: I am Ra. Quite.

QUESTIONER: What I am trying to get at is how these disciplines affect the energy centers and the power of the white magician. Will you tell me how that works?

RA: I am Ra. The heart of the discipline of the personality is threefold. One, know yourself. Two, accept yourself. Three, become the Creator.

The third step is that step which, when accomplished, renders one the most humble servant of all, transparent in personality and completely able to know and accept other-selves. In relation to the pursuit of the magical working, the continuing discipline of the personality involves the adept in knowing its self, accepting its self, and thus clearing the path towards the great indigo gateway to the Creator. To become the Creator is to become all that there is. There is, then, no personality in the sense with which the adept begins its learn/teaching. As the consciousness of the indigo ray becomes more crystalline, more work may be done; more may be expressed from intelligent infinity.

QUESTIONER: You stated that a working of service to others has the potential of alerting a great mass of light strength. Could you describe just exactly how this works and what the uses of this would be?

RA: I am Ra. There are sound vibratory complexes which act much like the dialing of your telephone. When they are appropriately vibrated with accompanying will and concentration, it is as though many upon your metaphysical or inner planes received a telephone call. This call they answer by their attention to your working.

QUESTIONER: There are many of these. The ones most obvious in our society are those used in the church rather than those used by the magical adept. What is the difference in the effect in those used in our various churches and those specifically magical incantations used by the adept?

RA: I am Ra. If all in your churches were adepts consciously full of will, of seeking, of concentration, of conscious knowledge of the calling, there would be no difference. The efficacy of the calling is a function of the magical qualities of those who call; that is, their desire to seek the altered state of consciousness desired.

QUESTIONER: In selecting the protective ritual, we finally agreed upon the Banishing Ritual of the Lesser Pentagram. I assume that these sound vibratory complexes are of the type of which you speak for the alerting of those on the inner planes. Is this correct?

RA: I am Ra. This is correct.

QUESTIONER: If we had constructed a ritual of our own with words used for the first time in this sequence of protection, what would have been the relative merit of this with respect to the ritual that we chose?

RA: I am Ra. It would be less. In constructing ritual, it is well to study the body of written work which is available for names of positive or service to others power are available.

QUESTIONER: I will make an analogy to the loudness of the ringing of the telephone in using the ritual as the efficiency of the practitioners using the ritual. I see several things affecting the efficiency of the ritual: first, the desire of the practitioners to serve, their ability to invoke the magical personality, their ability to visualize while performing the ritual, and let me ask you as to the relative importance of those items and how each may be intensified?

RA: I am Ra. This query borders upon over-specificity. It is most important for the adept to feel its own growth as teach/learner.
    We may only say that you correctly surmise the paramount import of the magical personality. This is a study in itself. With the appropriate emotional will, polarity, and purity, work may be done with or without proper sound vibration complexes. However, there is no need for the blunt instrument when the scalpel is available.

QUESTIONER: I assume that the reason that the rituals that have been used previously are of effect is that these words have built a bias in consciousness of those who have worked in these areas, so that those who are of a distortion of mind that we seek will respond to imprint in consciousness of this series of words. Is this correct?

RA: I am Ra. This is, to a great extent, correct. The exception is the sounding of some of what you call your Hebrew and some of what you call your Sanskrit vowels. These sound vibration complexes have power before time and space and represent configurations of light which built all that there is.

QUESTIONER: Why do these sounds have this property?

RA: I am Ra. The correspondence in vibratory complex is mathematical.
At this time, we have enough transferred energy for one full query.

QUESTIONER: How did the users of these sounds, Sanskrit and Hebrew, determine what these sounds were?

RA: I am Ra. In the case of the Hebrew, that entity known as Yahweh aided this knowledge through impression upon the material of genetic coding which became language, as you call it.
In the case of Sanskrit, the sound vibrations are pure due to the lack of previous, what you call, alphabet or letter naming. Thus the sound vibration complexes seemed to fall into place as from the Logos. This was a more, shall we say, natural or unaided situation or process.
We would at this time make note of the incident in the previous working where our contact was incorrectly placed for a short period and was then corrected. In the exercise of the fire you may see the initial spiral clockwise from the green-ray energy center, through the shoulders and head, then through the elbows, then to the left hand. The channel had been corrected before the remainder of this answer was completed.
Is there a brief query at this time?

QUESTIONER: Is there anything that we could do to make the instrument more comfortable or to improve the contact?

RA: I am Ra. All is well. The instrument continues in some pain, as you call this distortion. The neck area remains most distorted, although the changes have been, to a small degree, helpful. The alignments are good.

We would leave you now, my friends, in the love and in the light of the One Infinite Creator. Go forth, then, glorying and rejoicing in the power and in the peace of the One Infinite Creator. Adonai.

Session 75,
October 31, 1981

RA: I am Ra. I greet you in the love and in the light of the One Infinite Creator. We communicate now.

QUESTIONER: The instrument would like to know why twice during the "Benedictus" portion of the music, she sang in a group concert that she experienced what she believes to be a psychic attack?

RA: I am Ra. This is not a minor query.[*2] We shall first remove the notations, which are minor. In the vibrating, which you call singing, of the portion of what this instrument hallows as the Mass, which immediately precedes that which is the chink called the "Hosanna," there is an amount of physical exertion required that is exhausting to any entity. This portion of which we speak is termed the "Sanctus." We come now to the matter of interest.

When the entity Jehoshuah[*3] decided to return to the location called Jerusalem for the holy days of its people, it turned from work mixing love and wisdom and embraced martyrdom, which is the work of love without wisdom.

The "Hosanna," as it is termed, and the following "Benedictus," is that which is the written summation of what was shouted as Jehoshuah came into the place of its martyrdom. The general acceptance of this shout, "Hosanna to the son of David! Hosanna in the highest! Blessed is he who comes in the name of the Lord!," by that which is called the church has been a misstatement, an occurrence which has been, perhaps, unfortunate for it is more distorted than much of the so-called Mass.

There were two factions present to greet Jehoshuah; firstly, a small group of those which hoped for an earthly king. However, Jehoshuah rode upon an ass stating by its very demeanor that it was no earthly king and wished no fight with Roman or Sadducee.

---

*2. It may seem that there is an excessive amount of personal and rather melodramatic material about psychic attack included here. We considered long and hard before deciding not to delete it. Our reason: Ra seems to suggest that any "light worker" will, if successful in this work, attract some sort of negatively oriented greeting. Therefore, we wish to share our experiences and Ra's discussion of them, in hopes that the information might be helpful.

*3. Ra has previously identified this name as the name of Jesus in biblical times

The greater number were those which had been instructed by rabbi and elder to make jest of this entity, for those of the hierarchy feared this entity who seemed to be one of them, giving respect to their laws and then, in their eyes, betraying those time-honored laws and taking the people with it.

The chink for this instrument is this subtle situation which echoes down through your space/time and, more than this, the place the "Hosanna" holds as the harbinger of that turning to martyrdom. We may speak only generally here. The instrument did not experience the full force of the greeting, which it correctly identified during the "Hosanna," due to the intense concentration necessary to vibrate its portion of that composition. However, the "Benedictus" in this particular rendition of these words is vibrated by one entity. Thus the instrument relaxed its concentration and was immediately open to the fuller greeting.

QUESTIONER: The chink then, as I understand it, was originally created by the decision of Jesus to take the path of martyrdom? Is this correct?

RA: I am Ra. This is, in relation to this instrument, quite correct. It is aware of certain overbalances towards love, even to martyrdom, but has not yet, to any significant degree, balanced these distortions. We do not imply that this course of unbridled compassion has any fault, but affirm its perfection. It is an example of love which has served as beacon to many.

For those who seek further, the consequences of martyrdom must be considered, for in martyrdom lies the end of the opportunity, in the density of the martyr, to offer love and light. Each entity must seek its deepest path.

QUESTIONER: Let me see, then, if I understand how the Orion entity finds a chink in this distortion. The entity identifying in any amount toward martyrdom is then open by its free will to the aid of the Orion group to make it a martyr. Am I correct?

RA: I am Ra. You are correct only in the quite specialized position in which the instrument finds itself; that is, of being involved in and dedicated to work which is magical or extremely polarized in nature. This group entered this work with polarity but virtual innocence as to the magical nature of this polarity. That it is beginning to discover.

QUESTIONER: How was the Orion entity able to act through this linkage of the "Hosanna"? Was this simply because of mental distortions of the instrument at this period of time, because of that suggested by the music, or was it a more physical or metaphysical link from the time of Christ?

RA: I am Ra. Firstly, the latter supposition is false. This entity is not linked with the entity Jehoshuah. Secondly, there is a most unique circumstance. There is an entity which has attracted the attention of an Orion light being. This is extremely rare.

This entity has an intense devotion to the teachings and example of the one it calls Jesus. This entity then vibrates in song a most demanding version, called *The Mass in B Minor* by Bach, of this exemplary votive complex of sound vibrations. The entity is consciously identifying with each part of this Mass. Only thusly was the chink made available. As you can see, it is not an ordinary occurrence and would not have happened had any ingredient been left out: exhaustion, bias in the belief complexes, attention from an Orion entity, and the metaphysical nature of that particular set of words.

QUESTIONER: What was the Orion entity's objective with respect to the entity you spoke of who, in a demanding manner, sings the Mass?

RA: I am Ra. The Orion entity wishes to remove the instrument.

QUESTIONER: Is this a fourth or a fifth density?

RA: I am Ra. This instrument is being greeted by a fifth-density entity which has lost some polarity due to its lack of dictatorship over the disposition of the instrument's mind/body/spirit or its yellow-ray-activated physical complex.

QUESTIONER: You are speaking of this other person now who sang in the Mass? Is this correct?

RA: I am Ra. No.

QUESTIONER: I think there was a little miscommunication here. I was asking about the other person who sings the Mass in creating this chink that was also greeted by an Orion entity, and my question was what density is the Orion entity who greets the other person who sings the Mass?

RA: I am Ra. We did not speak of any entity but the instrument.

QUESTIONER: OK. I misunderstood. I thought you were speaking of someone else in the singing group who had been identified with the singing. The entire time we were speaking we were speaking only of the instrument? Is this correct?

RA: I am Ra. This is correct.

QUESTIONER: I am sorry for my confusion. Sometimes, as you say, sound vibration complexes are not very adequate.
The answer to this next question probably has to do with our distorted view of time, but as I see it, Wanderers in this density who come from the fifth density or sixth density should already be of a relatively high degree of adeptness, and they must follow a slightly different path back to the adeptness that they once had in a higher density and get as close to it as they can in the third density. Is this correct?

RA: I am Ra. Your query is less than perfectly focused. We shall address the subject in general.
There are many Wanderers whom you may call adepts who do no conscious work in the present incarnation. It is a matter of attention. One may be a fine catcher of your game sphere, but if the eye is not turned as this sphere is tossed, then perchance it will pass the entity by. If it turned its eyes upon the sphere, catching would be easy. In the case of Wanderers which seek to recapitulate the degree of adeptness which each had acquired previous to this life experience, we may note that even after the forgetting process has been penetrated, there is still the yellow-activated body which does not respond as does the adept which is of a green- or blue-ray-activated body. Thusly, you may see the inevitability of frustrations and confusion due to the inherent difficulties of manipulating the finer forces of consciousness through the chemical apparatus of the yellow-ray-activated body.

QUESTIONER: You probably can't answer this, but are there any suggestions that you could give with respect to the instrument's coming hospital experience that could be of benefit for her?

RA: I am Ra. We may make one suggestion and leave the remainder with the Creator. It is well for each to realize its self as the Creator. Thusly each may support each, including the support of self by humble love of self as Creator.

QUESTIONER: You spoke in a previous session about certain Hebrew and Sanskrit sound vibratory complexes being powerful because they were mathematically related to that which was the creation. Could you expand on this understanding as to how these are linked?

RA: I am Ra. As we previously stated, the linkage is mathematical or that of the ratio you may consider musical. There are those whose mind complex activities would attempt to resolve this mathematical ratio, but at present the coloration of the intoned vowel is part of the vibration, which cannot be accurately measured. However, it is equivalent to types of rotation of your primary material particles.

QUESTIONER: If these sounds are precisely vibrated, then what effect or use, with respect to the purposes of the adept, would they have?

RA: I am Ra. You may consider the concept of sympathetic resonance. When certain sounds are correctly vibrated, the creation sings.

QUESTIONER: Would these sounds, then, be of a musical nature in that there would be a musical arrangement of many different sound vibrations, or would this apply to just one single note? Which would it apply more to?

RA: I am Ra. This query is not easily answered. In some cases only the intoned vowel has effect. In other cases, most notably Sanskrit combinations, the selection of harmonic intervals is also of resonant nature.

QUESTIONER: Then would the adept use this resonant quality to become more one with the creation and, therefore, attain his objective in that way?

RA: I am Ra. It would be perhaps more accurate to state that in this circumstance, the creation becomes more and more contained within the practitioner. The balance of your query is correct.

QUESTIONER: Could you tell me the musical name of the notes to be intoned that are of this quality?

RA: I am Ra. We may not.

QUESTIONER: I didn't think that you could, but I thought it wouldn't hurt to ask.
Then I assume that these must be sought out and determined by empirical observation of their effect by the seeker. Is this correct?

RA: I am Ra. This is partially correct. As your seeking continues, there will be added to empirical data that acuity of sensibility which continued working in the ways of the adept offers.

QUESTIONER: Is the exercise of the fire best for the instrument, or is there anything better that we could do other than the things that you have already suggested to aid the instrument?

RA: I am Ra. Continue as you are at present. We cannot speak of the future, as we may then affect it, but there is a great probability/possibility if you follow the path which you now tread that more efficacious methods for the entire group will be established.

QUESTIONER: You mentioned in an earlier session that the hair was an antenna. Could you expand on that statement as to how that works?

RA: I am Ra. It is difficult to so do due to the metaphysical nature of this antennae effect. Your physics are concerned with measurements in your physical complex of experience. The metaphysical nature of the contact of those in time/space is such that the hair, as it has significant length, becomes as a type of electrical battery which stays charged and tuned and is then able to aid contact even when there are small anomalies in the contact.

QUESTIONER: Is there an optimum length of hair for this aid?

RA: I am Ra. There is no outer limit on length, but the, shall we say, inner limit is approximately 4 to 4-and-one-half inches depending upon the strength of the contact and the nature of the instrument.

QUESTIONER: May anyone in third density accomplish some degree of healing if they have the proper will, desire, and polarity, or is there a minimal balance of the energy centers of the healer that is also necessary?

RA: I am Ra. Any entity may at any time instantaneously clear and balance its energy centers. Thus, in many cases those normally quite blocked, weakened, and distorted may, through love and strength of will, become healers momentarily. To be a healer by nature, one must indeed train its self in the disciplines of the personality.

QUESTIONER: How does the use of the magical ritual invoking the magical personality aid the mind/body/spirit complex totality? Could you expand on the answer that you gave in the last session with respect to that?

RA: I am Ra. When the magical personality is properly and efficaciously invoked, the self has invoked its Higher Self. Thus a bridge betwixt space/time and time/space is made, and the sixth-density magical personality experiences directly the third-density catalyst for the duration of the working. It is most central to deliberately take off the magical personality after the working in order that the Higher Self resume its appropriate configuration as analog to the space/time mind/body/spirit.

QUESTIONER: Then you are saying that the act, signal, or key for the invoking of the magical personality which is the putting of something on or a gesture should also be as carefully taken off to reverse the gesture perhaps at the end of the invocation. Is this correct?

RA: I am Ra. This is correct. It should be fastidiously accomplished either in mind or by gesture as well if this is of significant aid.

QUESTIONER: Now in the invocation of the magical personality, it is not necessarily effective for the neophyte. Is there a point at which there is a definite quantum change and that then the magical personality does reside in the neophyte, or can it be done in small degrees or percentages of magical personality as the neophyte becomes more adept?

RA: I am Ra. The latter is correct.

QUESTIONER: The three aspects of the magical personality are stated to be power, love, and wisdom. Is this correct, and are these the only primary aspects of the magical personality?

RA: I am Ra. The three aspects of the magical personality, power, love, and wisdom, are so called in order that attention be paid to each aspect in developing the basic tool of the adept; that is, its self. It is by no means a personality of three aspects. It is a being of unity, a being of sixth density, and equivalent to what you call your Higher Self, and at the same time is a personality enormously rich in variety of experience and subtlety of emotion.

The three aspects are given that the neophyte not abuse the tools of its trade but rather approach those tools balanced in the center of love and wisdom and thus seeking power in order to serve.

QUESTIONER: Then is it correct that a good sequence for the developing of the magical personality would be alternate meditations, first on power, and then a meditation on love, and then a meditation on wisdom, and then to continue cycling that way?

RA: I am Ra. This is indeed an appropriate technique. In this particular group there is an additional aid in that each entity manifests one of these qualities in a manner which approaches the archetype. Thusly visualization may be personalized and much love and support within the group generated.

QUESTIONER: You made the statement in a previous session that the true adept lives more and more as it is. Will you explain and expand more upon that statement?

RA: I am Ra. Each entity is the Creator. The entity, as it becomes more and more conscious of its self, gradually comes to the turning point at which it determines to seek either in service to others or in service to self. The seeker becomes the adept when it has balanced with minimal adequacy the energy centers red, orange, yellow, and blue with the addition of the green for the positive, thus moving into indigo work.

The adept then begins to do less of the preliminary or outer work, having to do with function, and begins to effect the inner work, which has to do with being. As the adept becomes a more and more consciously crystallized entity, it gradually manifests more and more of that which it always has been since before time; that is, the One Infinite Creator.

This instrument begins to show rapid distortion towards increase of pain.

We, therefore, would offer time for any brief query before we leave this working.

QUESTIONER: Is there anything that we can do to make the instrument more comfortable or to improve the contact?

RA: I am Ra. You are conscientious. The alignments are well.

I am Ra. I leave you, my friends, in the love and the light of the One Infinite Creator. Go forth, therefore, rejoicing in the power and peace of the One Infinite Creator. Adonai.

INDEX

A

Aging, 61
Angels, 134
Ankh, 36
Archetypical mind, 7, 113, 127, 168–169
Ark of the covenant, 65–66
Astrology, 95
Atlantis, 49

B

Balance, 11, 15–16, 28, 37, 43, 45, 48, 69, 72, 123, 127,
    155–156, 170, 178–179
Bermuda triangle, 63
Bigfoot, 97
Biorhythms, 71
Blue, 31, 85
Brain, 13, 75
Brothers and sisters of sorrow, 16, 34, 101

C

Cancer, 66
Catalyst, 16, 26–30, 35–37, 46, 70–74, 87, 94, 96, 99–100,
    102, 104, 109, 117–118, 122, 127, 146, 162, 179
Cayce, Edgar, 101
Children, 87–88, 112
Colors, 10, 24–26, 40, 45, 92, 120, 123
Confederation (of planets in the service of the infinite cre-
    ator), 8, 19–23, 65, 67–68,104, 138
Council of Saturn, 67
Crystals, 51

D

Death, 10–12, 87–88, 106, 127, 130, 134–135, 143, 148
Densities:
   First, 82, 85, 91
   Second, 22, 82, 85, 91
   Third, 9, 15–16, 33–34, 50, 54–55, 57, 60, 64, 66–67, 69, 71, 74, 80, 82–83, 85–91, 94, 96, 99–100, 105–106, 109, 116–118, 123, 127, 131, 134–136, 143, 147–148, 162, 176, 179
   Fourth, 9, 13, 15, 50, 66, 80, 83, 86–91, 94, 103, 105–106, 109, 116–117, 143
   Fifth, 9, 13–15, 23, 50, 80–81, 94, 103, 105, 108, 120–124, 126, 129–130, 132, 143, 176
   Sixth, 9, 13–15, 35, 63–64, 93–94, 103, 105, 108, 127, 131, 143, 145, 152, 176, 179, 180
   Seventh, 15
Distortion, 26, 42, 46, 51, 54, 78, 111, 119, 131–132, 150, 156, 165

E

Earth changes, 45, 101–102, 104
Energy centers, 7, 10–11, 25–26, 28–32, 37, 40, 48, 51–52, 69, 74, 107–109, 113, 127, 151, 158, 160–162, 164, 169–170, 179, 181
Energy transfers & blockages, 10–11, 26, 30–31, 35, 38–39, 64, 66, 69, 75, 108, 110, 162, 165–166, 169
Etheric body, 112, 115
Evolution, physical, 90

F

Faith, 29, 31, 65, 128, 163
Forgetting, 16, 87–88, 103, 105–106, 177
Form–maker body, 12
Fourth, 9, 13, 50, 87, 94, 105, 143, 152
Free will, 12, 20, 26, 30, 57, 80, 91, 94, 100, 106, 110, 115, 122, 126, 132–134, 136–138, 142, 150, 155–156, 159–160, 162–163, 175

G

Green, 31
Guardians, Council of Saturn, 8, 123
Guardians, personal, 8

H

Hair, 133, 178–179
Harvest, 7–8, 16, 79, 90, 94, 103–104, 116–117, 127, 132, 143, 147
Healing, 31–32, 36–37, 39–44, 46, 51–52, 55–56, 58–60, 71–72, 74–75, 77, 96–97, 107–112, 115, 135, 144, 148–149, 161, 163–165, 179
Healing, allopathic, 78, 96
Hebrew, 172, 177
Higher Self, 8, 72, 127, 130, 135–137, 141–142, 148, 179–180
Hypnosis, 140

I

Indigo, 12, 31, 56
Inner Earth, 67
Inner planes, 8, 67, 90, 171
Intelligent energy, 12, 14, 24–26, 55–56, 75, 88, 110, 163
Intelligent infinity, 12, 31–32, 48, 50, 56, 75, 92, 100, 108, 127–128, 171

J

Jesus, 162–163, 174–175

L

Light, 8–9, 12–13, 15, 17–19, 23–26, 30–32, 37–39, 41, 43–44, 46–48, 50–51, 53–63, 70, 75–76, 80–83, 91–93, 95, 98, 101–103, 107, 110, 115, 118, 120, 122–126, 129, 133–134, 139, 144–148, 151, 153, 155–164, 167, 169, 171–173, 175, 181
Light/Love, 8, 93
Logos of the Milky Way Galaxy, 149
Love, 8, 12–13, 17–19, 23, 28, 30, 32–33, 38, 41, 43, 50–51, 56–57, 59, 62–63, 70, 72, 74–77, 80–85, 87, 89–93, 96, 98, 101–103, 107, 118, 120, 122–126, 129, 132–133, 135–137, 139, 145–146, 151, 153, 159, 167, 173–175, 177, 179–181

M

Magic, ritual, 34, 77, 92, 95, 121, 151, 179
Maldek, 57
Mars, 96, 169
Meditation, 7, 17, 32, 45, 48, 62, 64, 68, 74, 88, 110, 113,

115, 139, 147, 154, 165, 180
Messianic secret, 162–163
Metal–bending, 55–56, 87–88
Mind/Body/Spirit complexes, 8, 10–12, 14, 16–17, 19,
    24–32, 35, 38–39, 42–45, 56–57, 61, 65–66, 71, 75,
    78–79, 83, 87–91, 93–94, 101, 103–106, 108, 110–113,
    116, 120–121, 127, 130–136, 139, 141–145, 148, 154–
    157, 160–162, 165, 168–170, 176, 179
Mind/Body/Spirit Complex Totality, 8, 12, 179
Mummies, 69

N
90° deflection, 17

O
Orion group, 7, 9, 22–23, 42, 68, 79–80, 126, 136, 154, 175

P
Paranormal ability, 100
Planets, inhabited, 149
Polarization, 7, 16, 20–21, 28, 33, 88, 93, 101, 104, 113,
    116–117, 121, 127, 130–131, 133–134, 136–137, 147,
    149–151, 164
Prana, 38, 50, 59–61, 63, 108
Pre–incarnative choices, 165
Prophecy, 101–102
Psychic greeting, 158
Psychic surgery, 111
Pyramids, 35, 45, 47, 60, 63, 75, 106

R
Ra, 7–165, 167–173, 175–181
Rays, energy centers:
    Red, 29, 59, 83, 85, 181
    Orange, 29, 82–83, 85, 181
    Yellow, 83, 85, 181
    Green, 31
    Blue, 31,85
    Indigo, 12, 31, 56
    Violet, 40
Reincarnation, 86
Religion, 65, 66, 92, 171, 173, 174
Repression, 15

S
Sanskrit, 172–173, 177–178
Seniority of incarnation by vibration, 45, 70, 100
Service, 15–17, 22, 28, 34, 50, 54, 65, 68–69, 87, 92–93,
    96–100, 103, 106, 109, 111, 113, 116–117, 119–123,
    125–127, 129, 132, 135–136, 139–141, 146, 151–152,
    155, 157, 159, 164, 166, 171–172, 181
Sex, 22, 30, 34, 64, 72, 90, 97, 114–115,151, 166

T
Time/Space, 7, 11, 17, 35, 45, 48–50, 60, 77, 89, 99, 101–
    102, 111–112, 114–115, 120, 123, 130–131, 133–137,
    141–145, 147–149, 152–153, 156, 170, 179
Timelessness, 25

U
Ufos, 19
Unity, 17, 20, 50, 84, 93, 127, 145, 151, 180

V
Vibration, 8, 24–25, 45, 48, 50, 62, 70, 80, 82, 90, 100, 102,
    114, 118, 130, 143, 148, 150–151, 157, 165, 172–173,
    176–177

Vital energy, 49, 84, 92, 99, 140, 146, 153, 156–157, 159

W
Wanderers, 16, 19–21, 23, 57–58, 86–88, 99–100, 102–103,
    106, 118, 131, 137, 143, 176–177
War, 100
Water, 44, 54, 58, 63
Will, 8–17, 19–21, 23–35, 37–41, 43, 46, 49, 51–57, 60,
    62–63, 65–68, 72–77, 79–80, 82–91, 94–95, 97, 99–102,
    104–107, 110–122, 124, 126–128, 130, 132–138, 140,
    142–148, 150–153, 155–165, 168–172, 175, 177–180
Wisdom, 12, 16, 28, 72, 74, 80, 93, 96, 103, 125, 129, 174,
    180

Y
Yahweh, 65, 172

ABOUT THE AUTHORS

DON ELKINS was born in Louisville, Kentucky, in 1930. He held a BS and MS in mechanical engineering from the University of Louisville, as well as an MS in general engineering from Speed Scientific School. He was professor of physics and engineering at the University of Louisville for twelve years from 1953 to 1965. In 1965 he left his tenured position and became a Boeing 727 pilot for a major airline to devote himself more fully to UFO and paranormal research. He also served with distinction in the US Army as a master sergeant during the Korean War.

Don Elkins began his research into the paranormal in 1955. In 1962, Don started an experiment in channeling, using the protocols he had learned from a contactee group in Detroit, Michigan. That experiment blossomed into a channeling practice that led eventually to the Law of One material 19 years later. Don passed away on November 7, 1984.

CARLA L. RUECKERT (McCarty) was born in 1943 in Lake Forest, Illinois. She completed undergraduate studies in English literature at the University of Louisville in 1966 and earned her master's degree in library service in 1971.

Carla became partners with Don in 1968. In 1970, they formed L/L Research. In 1974, she began channeling and continued in that effort until she was stopped in 2011 by a spinal fusion surgery. During four of those thirty-seven years of channeling (1981–1984), Carla served as the instrument for the Law of One material.

In 1987, she married Jim McCarty, and together they continued the mission of L/L Research. Carla passed into larger life on April 1, 2015.

JAMES MCCARTY was born in 1947 in Kearney, Nebraska. After receiving an undergraduate degrees from the University of Nebraska at Kearney and a master of science in early childhood education from the University of Florida, Jim moved to a piece of wilderness in Marion County, Kentucky, in 1974 to build his own log cabin in the woods, and to develop a self-sufficient lifestyle. For the next six years, he was in almost complete retreat.

He founded the Rock Creek Research and Development Laboratories in 1977 to further his teaching efforts. After experimenting, Jim decided that he preferred the methods and directions he had found in studying with L/L Research in 1978. In 1980, he joined his research with Don's and Carla's.

Jim and Carla were married in 1987. Jim has a wide L/L correspondence and creates wonderful gardens and stonework. He enjoys beauty, nature, dance, and silence.

NOTE: The Ra contact continued until session number 106. There are five volumes total in The Law of One series, Book I–Book V. There is also other material available from our research group on our archive website, www.llresearch.org.

You may reach us by email at contact@llresearch.org, or by mail at: L/L Research, P.O. Box 5195, Louisville, KY 40255–0195

NOTES

NOTES